EAT YOUR FRONT GARDEN

Dedicated to Mum and Colin, with love.

THE ENGLISH KITCHEN

Eat Your Front Garden

Mat Coward

PROSPECT BOOKS

2020

This edition published in 2020 in Great Britain and the USA by Prospect Books at 26 Parke Road, London, SW13 9NG

© 2020, text and photographs by Mat Coward.

British Library Cataloguing in Publication Data:
A catalogue entry for this book is available from the British Library.

ISBN 13: 978-1-909248-67-0

Printed by the Gutenberg Press Ltd., Malta.

TABLE OF CONTENTS

Introduction   7

Section One: plants grown mainly for their flowers

Dahlia   13

Daylily   25

Canna   33

Mallow   39

Amaranth   45

Garlic chives   55

Sunflower   63

Bellflower   69

Stridolo   75

Section Two: plants grown mainly for their foliage

Japanese ginger   81

Bamboo   87

Perilla   93

Earth chestnut   99

Red orach   103

Chop suey greens   107

Tiger nuts   113

Rock samphire   121

Chinese water celery   131

Section Three: plants grown mainly as climbers

Mashua 139

Apios 151

Chinese yam 159

Caucasian spinach 165

Vine leaves 171

Hop shoots 177

Section Four: plants grown mainly for ground cover

Crosnes 185

Nasturtium 191

Oca 197

Hosta 205

Section Five: plants grown mainly as hedging

Japanese quince 215

Honeyberry 221

Fuchsia 227

Section Six: resources

A selection of seed & plant suppliers 234

Sundry suppliers 234

Further reading 235

Index

Index 236

Introduction

There are neighbourhoods in the world where people are forbidden by law from growing vegetables in their front gardens. Those who do so can be charged with committing a misdemeanour, and even, in theory, jailed. In some places you can not only be compelled to put your front garden down to lawn, but even to keep it mown to a specified, statutory height.

Here in Britain, we perhaps live in a generally more liberal state, with greater tolerance of eccentricity. Even so, I once a knew a man who was ordered by his landlord to stop growing carrots in the window boxes of his rented flat because vegetables 'made the property look scruffy'. (I'm glad to say that he replaced the carrots with nasturtiums, which are just about the most wholly edible plants on earth.)

But although in this country we don't need to fear a knock on the door from a local authority enforcement officer, there are still plenty of reasons why people might be shy about openly filling their front gardens with vegetables.

Most obviously, there's simple conformism. If all your neighbours plant up their fronts with grass and shrubs, or cover them with tarmac and shingle, you might feel that devoting yours to broccoli and onions, spuds and beans, would mark you out as *odd*. We British might tolerate eccentricity – but only in other people, thank you, not in ourselves.

There are more practical objections, too. If your front garden looked like a vegetable patch, would that have an undesirable effect on the price of your property, or – mortifyingly – the price of your neighbour's property? Would out-front cabbages be tempting to passing thieves or vandals? And then, of course, there are plenty of tenants with unsympathetic landlords, such as my friend with the carrots.

At the same time, I know a lot of people who would like to grow some food in the front – because their front garden is sunnier or more sheltered than their back garden, or because the back isn't big enough to feed their family and they've already spent three years on the waiting list for an allotment, or because they are 'grow-your-own' fanatics who grind their teeth in frustration every time they think of all that wasted space. Or simply because the front garden is the only garden they've got.

This book, and the idea of the 'invisible allotment', is aimed at all those people. It offers some suggestions for edible plants that can easily be smuggled into ostensibly ornamental gardens, as well as detailed advice on how to grow and eat them. These are crops that you can grow without scandalising the neighbours. Your front garden won't look like an allotment, but you'll still get a significant amount of food out of it.

There are plants here which are *bona fide*, universally acknowledged 'ornamentals' – sold and grown for looking at – but which, to many people's surprise, have edible parts. You may well have some of these plants in your front garden already, which will give you a head start (and save a few quid).

Then there are species which are grown as ornamentals in this country, but which are considered vegetables back in their homelands. Hosta is a good example: in Japan it's grown as an agricultural crop, here as a herbaceous perennial with colourful leaves.

Finally, I've included some lesser-known edible plants which *would* be used as ornamentals in UK gardens, if they were used at all, such as the Cinnamon Vine (*Dioscorea batatas*) which is a charmingly-perfumed climber – and as long as you don't tell anyone that one of its other names is Chinese Yam, then only *you* need ever know that every now and then you're going to dig up its roots and roast them.

In order that you can look for a plant to fill a gap in your front garden, while knowing that it will also provide a crop for your invisible allotment, the book is divided into sections that relate to the plant's ornamental use, rather than its edible use. Dahlia, for instance, is listed in the section dealing with plants mainly grown for their flowers, though it's the tubers that you actually eat.

Perhaps I should finish by briefly explaining what I *haven't* put in this book. I haven't included what might be called 'vegetables that look nice'. In my view, as a dedicated vegetable grower, all vegetables look nice. And, for the most part, I haven't included herbs used purely for flavouring. The plants in this book must meet two criteria: they need to be substantially, not just peripherally, edible; and they need to be unobtrusive when grown in a front garden.

In other words – we're not planting a potager. We're planting an invisible allotment.

Note

If you're gardening outside the UK, to adjust the dates mentioned in the book to suit local conditions please note that the UK gardening calendar goes as follows:

Early spring: March	Early summer: June
Mid-spring: April	Mid-summer: July
Late spring: May	Late summer: August
Early autumn: September	Early winter: December
Mid-autumn: October	Mid-winter: January
Late autumn: November	Late winter: February.

Readers used to USDA Hardiness Zones may like to know that the area in which I garden is considered approximately equivalent to Zone 8.

Flower spike of amaranth (*Amaranthus*)

SECTION ONE

PLANTS GROWN MAINLY FOR THEIR FLOWERS

Dahlia bloom

Dahlia (*Dahlia*)

I've often read that the dahlia was originally brought to Europe from its native Mexico as a vegetable, but that over the years plant breeders concentrated on making the flowers more beautiful rather than on making the tubers more tasty, until eventually the dahlia crossed over entirely from one category to another, from vegetable to ornamental. I've never seen a solid source for that history, so I remain sceptical. But what's not in doubt is that dahlias have been used as food (and indeed medicine) for thousands of years – and that they are among the UK's most popular and reliable garden plants. Dahlias are tuberous perennials; their hardiness varies.

Ornamental value

Dahlias grown in the UK are visible in the garden from late spring until early autumn, disappearing during the frosty months. They're bushy plants, ranging in height from about 2 feet (0.6 m) to 5 feet (1.5 m), and spreading sideways from about 15 inches (38 cm) to 3 feet (1 m), with (in most cases) green leaves – but there are dozens of species of dahlia, and many thousands of cultivars, which makes any generalisation about them a bit risky.

The flowers, which are in bloom from late spring or early summer until the first autumn frost, come in an assortment of shapes, sizes, and colours: yellow, red, pink, orange, white, bicoloured, and more. Bees – especially bumblebees – work them steadily. Dahlias make handsome cut flowers, and last the longest if picked in the cool of early morning or late evening.

Hoverfly feeding on dahlia

How to start

I like to start with a packet of seed – it's cheap, simple, and satisfying – but you could also buy tubers or young plants, or take cuttings from existing plants.

Dahlia seed germinates very easily. In March or April, fill a 3 inch (7.5 cm) plastic flowerpot with seed compost, or peat-free multipurpose compost. (It doesn't have to be 3 inches, incidentally, it doesn't have to be plastic, and it doesn't even have to be a flower pot; it could be a small seed tray, a large pot, or indeed an empty family-sized yoghurt container with a hole stabbed in the bottom. Instructions such as these are only made so precise for simplicity's sake.) Stand the pot in a saucer of water for a few minutes, until its contents are moist, but not dripping wet. Now place about four seeds on the surface of the compost, and cover them over with more

EAT YOUR FRONT GARDEN

compost (i.e. taken from the bag, not from the pot), so that they are buried about an ⅛ of an inch (3 mm) deep.

It's a good idea to cover the pot, to keep the compost from drying out. An inflated plastic food bag held in place with a rubber band will do, though I find the sliced-off base of a plastic water bottle is simpler. But anything more or less airtight and transparent is fine. Put the pot somewhere reasonably light and warm. The windowsill of any room in your house should be OK. Dahlia seeds usually germinate within a week or so, and often in just a few days. Make sure to check regularly, because you need to remove the cover as soon as the first seedling appears.

Once the seedlings in the pot have grown so much that they are touching each other, it's time to delicately prick them out into individual pots, in peat-free multipurpose compost, using a tool called a dibber, or perhaps the tip of a penknife (or maybe a dead biro – haven't you always wanted to find a use for dead biros?). The pots should now stand somewhere with full daylight, but not too warm – an unheated greenhouse or conservatory is best, but a bright windowsill in a cool room will serve. As the young plants fill their pots, so that there are roots showing through the drainage holes underneath, move them on to a slightly bigger pot.

Growing from seed, you can't be quite certain what you're going to get. I find that interesting, because it allows me to grow a number of dahlias and then choose which ones I want to keep at the end of the season, based on which of the plants are best looking, most palatable, and the strongest growers. For instance, I have a dislike of salmon pink flowers (I don't know why, perhaps I was bitten by a fish as a child), so when one of those comes up from seed, I'll eat all its tubers in the autumn, instead of keeping any for replanting. At the time of planting out dahlia plants you can apparently tell what colour the blooms will be: pale green stems mean white or yellow flowers; amber-flushed stems are peach, rose and orange; dark crimson or bronze stems are maroon, crimson or scarlet.

As far as anyone knows, all dahlias are edible, but not all are pleasant to eat. There are some which are widely recommended for eating, and if you prefer someone else to do the experimenting you can find these online. In particular there's a company called Lubera (see Resources, pages 234-5) which has run trials to select a small range of dahlias that have the best flavours and the least fibrous flesh. Their website describes the flowering and eating qualities of each, and sells them as young plants. Generally, it's said that cactus-flowered types are reliably good eaters.

In late winter and early spring, tubers, plants and seeds are available from hundreds of online shops and dahlia specialists, seed and plant catalogues, garden centres, nurseries and supermarkets. But if you've a friend who's got a dahlia, you could just take a cutting from that.

There are many different ways of storing and of propagating dahlias, which can easily be found on the internet or in the library if you want to experiment with different methods. To avoid confusion – or, if I'm being too optimistic here, at least to *reduce* confusion – I'm only going to describe (both here, and in the section on Harvest & Storage, below) the routine I have ended up using, after trying various methods over the years. Dahlias are really very easy to propagate and to keep going, so if this method doesn't work for you then don't give up, just look up another system and try that. I can almost guarantee you'll eventually find one that suits you; this is *not* a difficult plant.

In March or April I take the clump of tubers that I want to propagate from out of storage, and set it in a large seed tray of moist compost, so that the plump, sausagey tubers themselves are mostly covered, but the 'crown' – the bit in the middle where all the tubers join the remains of last year's stem – is above the level of the compost. Keep the tray somewhere light and at the sort of

Dahlia blooms and flower buds

temperature you might find in a spare bedroom – about 60-65 °F (16-18 °C).

After a while, probably a fortnight or so, buds will appear low down on the crown. They're usually referred to as 'eyes', which is both creepy and undescriptive; what they actually are is little bumps. It's from these buds that this year's new, green growth will eventually come, so when you divide the clump you must make sure that each piece has at least one bud. It must also have at least one 'sausage', and a piece of the old stem. Got that? One eye, one sausage, half a stump.

In practice, if you just cut the clump in half, straight down through the middle of the old stem, you'd be very unlucky not to come away with two valid pieces. That, admittedly, can be harder work than it sounds. The usual advice in books is to use a 'clean, sharp knife', but these clumps, well-grown, can be big and tough, and I often end up sawing them in half as if they were logs for the fire.

Having done that, and had a bit of a sit-down, I then plant the two halves into the smallest size of pot that will take them, using peat-free multipurpose compost, at a depth which leaves the buds or shoots just peeping out. (If you have trouble identifying the buds, just wait a bit longer until you see the shoots start, and then proceed as above.)

Growing

Whether started from seed, plant, tuber or cutting, your dahlias are ready to plant out into their final positions once there is no further risk of frost, in late spring or early summer.

There's very little that will dissuade a dahlia from growing, and I've known them to grow perfectly well in poor soil in partial shade, but if you can find them a spot in full sun, in soil that's rich and deep, they'll do even better. The tubers, even more than the flowers, will benefit greatly from ground that's had a few bucketfuls of garden compost forked or raked into it a few weeks earlier. The one thing dahlias won't tolerate is soil that gets waterlogged.

Each dahlia needs about 2 to 3 feet (60 cm to 1 m) of horizontal space to grow in, the exact amount depending on the type of dahlia, and how you grow it. Dig a hole and plant the dahlia in it, so that when the hole is refilled the tubers are about six inches below the soil. If you're using bought-in plants, plant them at the same level as they were in their pots. Water the area thoroughly with a watering can; this isn't for the sake of moisture so much as for settling the plants into their holes, by getting rid of air pockets.

The final job on planting day is one you really don't want to skimp on: staking the plants. Even short dahlias will grow quite tall, and by late summer they'll be heavy with branches and flowers, and will be vulnerable to being knocked over by any decent summer gale, or even losing limbs to the weight of water after a downpour. So put a bamboo pole or, preferably, a wooden stake about a foot (30 cm) away from the tubers, pushing or hammering it in so that it's firmly anchored in the ground. At least 18 inches (45 cm) of the stake should be below ground if possible. As the plant grows, tie it to this pole with garden twine (or old shoelaces) at intervals.

It's impossible to exaggerate how important this staking is. If, when you've finished staking the young plants, you've got what looks like embarrassingly comical overkill, then you've done it right. If you've stopped short of the laugh-out-loud stage then you haven't done enough and your plants will fall over in September, unless they've already fallen over in August.

Dahlias respond well to regular watering throughout the summer – in particular, this helps prevent the edible tubers becoming too fibrous. Beware of over-feeding the plants, which is likely to produce a lot of growth above ground and little below. My soil is fairly rich to start with, so I don't use any fertiliser on my dahlias other than the compost mentioned earlier.

This is a plant that grows well in containers. Choose a tub large enough that its compost won't dry out quickly in hot weather. One with a capacity of about 30 litres (the volume will usually be marked on the bottom or side of the pot) filled with peat-free multipurpose compost should be OK. Having said that, they'll do quite well in surprisingly small containers, as I found out one year when I had far too many plants and never got round to finding spaces for them all. Some of them spent the whole summer in 6 inch (15 cm) deep mushroom trays or 10 inch (25 cm) pots, and they still managed to produce plentiful blooms and a fair crop of tubers.

Some experimenters have found that tuber growth in dahlias can be significantly increased if you prevent the plants from flowering, by removing the buds before they open. I think you'd have to be pretty desperate for food to do that, and in any case it would be unsuitable advice in a book dedicated to the invisible allotment. I never remove any flowers, and always have a good crop of tubers.

I do deadhead my dahlias, cutting off the finished flowers, on the assumption that by preventing the plants from setting seeds I'm forcing them to make further flowers, but there's no need to do that if you don't want to or haven't got time. Or – let's be frank – can't be bothered. From the point of view of this book, the flowers exist mainly to disguise the vegetable beneath (*snigger, chortle, the fools have no idea, etc*), but if the mood takes you, you can spend half the summer messing around with your dahlias. Some growers, for instance, 'stop' the plants – removing the tips of the main stems three weeks after planting in order to increase bushiness. 'Disbudding' means taking off the flower buds on the sides of the stems, leaving only the ones at the top, which should give you fewer, larger blooms.

PROBLEMS

I've never had any problems with dahlias, except for them toppling over in the wind, as mentioned above. I've heard that slugs will eat very young plants, in which case the obvious answer is to keep them indoors a bit longer before planting them out, so that by the time they go out they are too big to be of interest to the slugs.

Petals and leaves can be nibbled by various creatures – most notoriously the earwig – but seriously, name *one* person you know who's got enough time on their hands to worry about that? Of course if you're planning to enter your flowers for a show, you'll want them to be perfect, but if that's the case then I'm afraid they've sent you the wrong book and you need to contact customer services.

There are a number of diseases that can attack dahlias, but either I've never had any that have suffered in this way, or else I've never had any badly affected enough for me to actually notice. Either way, I'm not qualified to advise you on what to do if your dahlias look unwell – instead, I would recommend the very clear guide to pests and diseases on the website of the National Dahlia Society (www.dahlia-nds.co.uk).

In general, the dahlia is a resilient plant, rarely troubled to a severe degree by pests or diseases.

HARVEST & STORAGE

When the leaves of the dahlia are blackened by the first frosts of autumn, cut all the stems down with secateurs, so that just 4-6 inches (10-15 cm) remains. Dig up the whole plant using a spade or large garden fork, going carefully so as not to damage outlying tubers.

In a cool, dry place, such as a garage or shed, turn the clump upside down and leave it that way for at least a fortnight to help it dry. What I do is crunch some chicken wire into an open ball shape, so that the remains of the stems poking through the holes in the wire hold the clump in position. An old bicycle basket or bottle crate, upside down, would perform the same role.

After that period, the mud clinging to the clump should be dry enough to be gently rubbed away without damaging the tubers; it doesn't need to be spotless, just get the worst of it off.

At this point, I select the tubers that I'm going to use for food, slicing them off from the clumps. Any that are damaged I'll take for immediate use, because they're less likely to store well. Other than that, I choose ones that feel plump and firm, and are of medium size – not the giants and not the tiddlers.

Dahlia tubers – from *my* garden, that is – come in various shapes and sizes, ranging from very oblong to almost round, from 2 to 3 inches (5 cm to 7.5 cm) wide, and up to about 6 inches (15 cm) long. The heaviest individual tubers weigh around 9 ounces (255 g), while my most productive dahlias will give a total annual weight of about 4 lbs (1.80 kg) per plant.

I store the eaters in boxes full of horticultural sand (see Resources, pages 234-5), buried so that no part of them is exposed to the air, and spaced within the boxes so that no tuber is touching another. In a cool place they should keep for months like that, ready to be taken out for eating as needed.

To overwinter the remaining clumps, for replanting next year, I do much the same, burying them, with just their old stems showing, in pots of clean peat-free multipurpose compost, in the proverbial cool, dry place. A garage is probably the best option, but sheds, greenhouses and cool spare rooms are also used. In February or March I'll move these pots to somewhere warmer and lighter to start them into new growth.

Eating

Always start by peeling the tubers, as any bitterness or stringiness is most likely to be found just under the skin. From there, you can use them like potatoes, roasted, grated for latkes or rosti, boiled, steamed, mashed and fried. Or use them as if they were root vegetables in slow-cooked dishes such as stews, casseroles and pies. Dahlia can be either an ingredient or a side vegetable. Some people eat them raw, thinly sliced and salted in salads. They're sometimes used for sweet purposes: they can be grated for a version of carrot cake, and a syrup is extracted from them which can be made into a hot drink.

You can find all sorts of flavours in dahlia, though perhaps only if you're looking for them. I've read references to chocolate, coffee, every imaginable root and tuber crop, asparagus, parsley and many more. It's hard to think of any vegetable which varies so widely in flavours between different varieties and cultivars, from sweet to sour and from earthy to sharp, so it's worth trying as many types as

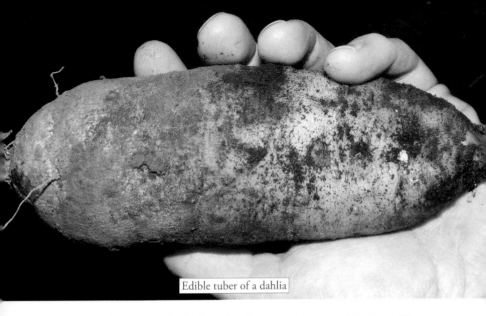

Edible tuber of a dahlia

you can find room for before deciding on those you like best. The texture of the tubers also varies: some are crisp and firm, a bit like mooli radish, and some are softer, more like spuds.

Dahlia tubers may become more fibrous as they get older and bigger, so you might want to change your methods of cooking to take this into account when using younger, smaller tubers from the outside of the clump, as opposed to the big old ones towards the middle. Also, like many tuberous crops, dahlias often become sweeter in storage.

Speaking of which, the main storage carbohydrate in dahlia is inulin, which some people find troublesome to the digestion. If you've ever had an upset stomach from eating too many Jerusalem artichokes, for instance, you would be wise to eat dahlia in cautious amounts at first.

The petals of dahlias are also edible. I can't say I find them especially flavoursome, but they do look very cheerful scattered over a salad or a rice dish.

Flowers and buds of daylily (*Hemerocallis*)

DAYLILY (*HEMEROCALLIS*)

*Also known as: Jin zhen cai, Golden needles, Yellow flower
vegetable, Gum zum, Huang hua cai, ditch lilies.*

Daylily is a clump-forming hardy perennial, mostly herbaceous,
though a few varieties keep some of their greenery in winter. In
temperate climates like ours it's become one of the commonest front
garden flowers due to its showy blooms, and because it's so easy
to grow. In much of Asia, especially China, it's better known as a
farmed crop and a staple kitchen ingredient.

It's very important that you buy this plant by its botanical name,
rather than its common name, since it isn't a real lily and most actual
lilies are inedible or even poisonous.

ORNAMENTAL VALUE

In this country, daylily's popularity is due to its excellent, lily-like
flowers (most commonly yellow or red), which are quite large,
velvety, and rather luxurious. They only last for a day or two, but
are rapidly replaced and produced in good numbers. The plants will
flower for a month or so during the summer.

The foliage is stiff, arching and strap-like, with most varieties
reaching a height of 1-3 feet (30-90 cm).

HOW TO START

Plants in pots are widely on sale in spring and summer. They should be planted in the garden or into containers after the last spring frosts, at the same depth they were in their original pots. Bare roots are also sold in garden centres; these need planting in pots initially, and are then kept in a cold frame or unheated greenhouse until they're growing strongly, for planting out in spring or autumn.

You can propagate existing daylilies in spring or autumn by digging up the whole lot, and dividing them into clumps that have both roots and shoots. The clumps can be hard work – saw them apart if necessary. Replant at the same level they were previously growing, that is with the crown of the plant just below the soil – if it's planted too deep it may rot. Place them about 18 inches (46 cm) apart.

Hemerocallis is very easy to grow from fresh seed, but it's not always easy to find fresh seed. I bought mine from a specialist grower on the internet one autumn and kept them in the fridge, in an envelope, until the following spring, when I sowed them in small pots in an unheated greenhouse. Dried seed is widely available, but can be very slow to germinate – you should wait at least six months before giving up on them. Sow the seeds in mid-spring in individual pots in peat-free multipurpose compost, and keep them under cover in an unheated greenhouse or similar. Grow them on under cover for their first year to let them get established, then plant them out the following May.

There are about twenty species and many thousands of cultivars of daylily, and as far as anyone knows all are edible, though some will be more palatable than others. In 2004, the US Department of Agriculture Research Service published a paper on daylily as a potential food which reported that 'All parts of the daylily (*Hemereocallis sp.*) are edible', and that, in its trials, the cultivar named Rosie Meyer was the most preferred for eating. The species *H. fulva* is often recommended for bud production, while *H. citrina*

Clump of daylily (*Hemerocallis*) alongside a wall

seems to be the main source of 'golden needles' (see below) in China. Stella De Oro (sometimes listed as Stella D'Oro), famous for its long blooming season, is very widely sold, and is often mentioned as being one of the best to eat.

GROWING

The daylily is so remarkably unfussy about its growing conditions that in some parts of the world it grows as a weed, having escaped from gardens. I've yet to find a soil or a position in which it won't survive. It tolerates shade, dry soil, and even damp soil. If you've got a sunny, dry patch where nothing thrives, try daylily there – and it's also a useful plant for heavy clay soil. However, as an ornamental vegetable it will be at its best in full sun, in fertile and well-drained soil.

I grow them successfully in 30 litre tubs, but whenever they're in containers you do need to keep an eye on the drainage holes for emerging roots. Daylilies seem to become rootbound easily and quickly, and I've often had to cut them out of pots, either to pot them on or to propagate them, even in their first year from seed. Move them on as soon as the roots start showing.

Despite their tolerance of dry soil, they do need plenty of watering, especially when you plant them out, and a mulch of compost in spring is advisable to retain moisture through the summer. They'll survive a drought, even when neglected, but you won't get so many flowers.

Apart from watering, they need very little maintenance. Only feed them (with a general purpose fertiliser) if you find they're not growing satisfactorily – otherwise they're best left alone to get on with it.

The browned, dead leaves can be removed (by tugging rather than cutting them) in autumn, or when growth restarts in spring.

Problems

Daylily reputedly suffers from slug attacks to its young foliage in early spring, though I've never seen that happen. If this proves to be a problem in your garden, then you might be better growing them in containers rather than the open ground.

Hemerocallis is otherwise not much prone to pests or diseases, with one exception. If you find that the flowers aren't opening, and perhaps have a distorted look to them, this probably means they're suffering from Hemerocallis gall midge, which develops inside the flower buds as a grub. The bad news is there's nothing much you can do about it. The good news is you don't need to do anything much about it, except wait: by mid-July the creature will have completed its life cycle, and subsequent flowers will develop normally.

HARVEST & STORAGE

For several weeks during the summer large numbers of buds and flowers are produced each day. If you grow a range of species, you may be able to harvest from late spring to early autumn.

As a general rule, harvest buds in the morning (when they are plump and full, and before they start to open), flowers at the end of the day (when fully open), and withered flowers the next morning. I find that the fresh flowers don't keep well at all, and are best used the same day. Buds will keep in bags in the fridge for a week. Wilted flowers, once picked, should be left exposed to the sun, for instance on a kitchen windowsill, until the next day, when they are traditionally dried for future use.

Both flowers and buds can be dried. In our climate, I've found that it's best to use a dehydrator, rather than simply stringing them up in the sun as they do in hotter, drier places.

EATING

Both the buds and the flowers of daylily are tasty, and surprisingly substantial.

The buds are an inch or so (2.5 cm) long (depending on the variety), oval and pale green. They have a crisp texture, and taste something like French beans or sugar snap peas – in fact, they are often used as if they were French beans. They need no preparation beyond washing, and can be eaten raw or, for the fullest flavour, steamed or stir-fried for a few minutes. Many reports suggest that raw flowers and buds (as opposed to cooked or dried) can cause a

Edible flower buds of daylily (*Hemerocallis*)

reaction in some people in the form of digestive upset, a burning in the throat, or a bitter aftertaste. In any case when you're eating something new to you, it's common sense to eat it nervously at first, nibbling rather than feasting, until you're certain it doesn't disagree with you.

Dried buds and flowers are sold in Chinese shops worldwide as 'golden needles', an important ingredient in many Chinese recipes, including one pan-Asian dish everyone's heard of: hot and sour soup. You'll find golden needles listed in lots of recipes online and in cookery books.

The best daylily flowers have a slightly peppery, perfumed flavour. They are sometimes used raw in salads, or fried in batter. Fresh, they're quite crunchy and sweet. Yesterday's flowers, wilted overnight, become limp, chewy, savoury rather than sweet. They are really good (as always) in stir-fries, but best of all I think in soups, where they take on a texture something like dried mushrooms.

Dried flowers are employed as a thickener in many dishes, and historically were used by vegetarian monks to give a meaty savour and chewiness to soups and stews.

In some places, other parts of the plant are eaten, though I've never tried them. Many sources of information give warnings that they can be indigestible in large quantities, which I must admit has always put me off a bit. Besides, the flowers and buds are produced so bountifully, and with so little effort, that I don't really feel motivated to explore further.

Canna, growing in a potato grow-bag

CANNA (*CANNA EDULIS* OR *CANNA INDICA*)

Also known as: Indian shot plant, Achira, Queensland arrowroot, Canna lily. Authorities differ over whether C. edulis is a species, or if it's a synonym for, or a form of, C. indica.

A summer bedding plant in British gardens, canna is often grown both for its long, green, and sometimes bronzed leaves – which begin as furled angels' trumpets before unfolding into a spear shape – and for its large, exotic-looking flowers. A half-hardy, slowly spreading perennial, canna also has starchy rhizomes which are an important food crop in some parts of the world.

ORNAMENTAL VALUE

Canna resembles a banana plant in its tropical lushness; it looks like something you'd find growing under humid glass at Kew, rather than in the beds next to the bowls club in the local park. The types used for eating often have smaller and less showy flowers than the purely ornamental varieties, but this is still a particularly attractive item. In this country it'll grow to be about 5 feet (1.5 m) tall.

HOW TO START

Canna is very easy to grow from seed, either bought or collected, but the best plants seem to come from divisions, not sowings. On the other hand starting them from seed is cheap and enjoyable.

In late winter or early spring, as soon as you can guarantee a constant temperature of around 68 °F (20 °C), put the seeds into warm water and leave them to soak for 48 hours. By then, they should have swollen visibly and softened a little. Sow them individually, one or two inches (2.5 cm) deep, in small pots of peat-free multipurpose or seed compost, and place the pots in good light at ordinary room temperature. The seeds will take anything from three weeks to two months to germinate.

Keep an eye on the bottom of the pots as the seedlings grow. If roots show through the drainage holes, move the plants on to slightly larger pots. They'll grow quite quickly at this stage, and by May they should be 6 inches (15 cm) tall.

For more reliable plants with a better chance of producing good flowers, buy rhizomes in late winter. Pot them up in late March and grow them on under cover – they don't need heat, just protection from frost and rain. Use peat-free multipurpose compost in a pot of about 6-10 inches (15-25 cm), with the rhizome just covered by compost. If shoots are present, leave them showing above the surface. Water very lightly – overwatered rhizomes will rot. Increase the watering as the foliage develops, but always conservatively until the plants are in their final positions.

To divide existing plants, whether left in the ground or stored in a shed over winter, wait until they start coming back into growth in spring. You can then cut the clump into as many pieces as there are growing points – each new piece must have at least one growing point on it, preferably two or three. Pot them up separately and keep them under shelter until you're sure they are properly established and are growing vigorously, then plant them out. As a rule, only divide canna when you need to – for propagation, or to make room – because bigger clumps tend to make bigger plants.

Most conveniently and reliably of all, and most expensively, you can buy growing plants at any time of year.

Growing

Try to find canna a spot in full sun, not only because it thrives in the light but also because any overhanging foliage might cause the soil to dry out. It is best in rich, deep soil, with plenty of compost or manure in it.

When planting out in spring after the last frosts, put the rhizomes 3-5 inches (7.5-13 cm) below the surface, and about 1 foot (30 cm) apart. Canna might need staking if planted in a windy position, but they're sturdy, upright plants on the whole. Cut off the dying flowers regularly to keep new ones coming. Applying a liquid fertiliser, such as seaweed extract, once or twice during the summer should also help. In hot weather water freely. Canna grow well in containers, but need good-sized pots – at least 1 foot (30 cm) across, and the bigger the better. Plant them in pots just as you would in the ground, but remember they'll need more feeding and watering.

Problems

This is a vigorous plant which smothers the weeds around it. It isn't subject to many diseases, and the only animals likely to bother it are slugs and snails eating its very early growth, and occasionally birds breaking off the young foliage – I've never seen them in the act, so I don't know whether they are pecking at the leaves to eat them, or snapping them off when they try to perch on them. Whichever it is, a temporary arrangement of short sticks with cotton strung between them, will make it hard for the birds to get at the plants during their vulnerable stage.

A failure to flower is probably the most common and obvious problem with canna. If you're growing from seed, you may just have to be patient – with luck, the plants will flower the following year. Otherwise, insufficiently fertile soil, or a lack of watering, or just bringing the rhizomes back into growth too late in the year, may all contribute to a lack of blooms. You could try to fix any of those problems, or you could just reclassify your canna as foliage plants, and therefore declare them a success.

Harvest & Storage

It's the younger rhizomes that are best for eating – the larger, older ones can be too fibrous. They can be harvested during the summer, any time when they're big enough to be worth bothering with, but in our climate it's usual to leave them until the first frost kills the foliage, and then lift the whole plant out of the ground with a garden fork. If you've got several clumps, it would be interesting to experiment by sampling rhizomes at different times in summer and autumn, to find when they are at their best in your garden conditions and according to your taste.

Overwinter canna rhizomes for eating and for replanting, just as you would dahlias (see pages 13-23). Many gardeners leave the plants in the ground for the winter, under a 6 inch (15 cm) mulch of compost or bark chips to keep the worst of the frost off, and find that they survive to reappear the following year. This is probably only worth trying if you have very free-draining soil; as with so many plants that get killed by our winters, it's not the cold itself that does them in, but the waterlogging.

If you're growing them in containers, all you've got to do is move the whole pot to somewhere frost-free for winter. Of course, you can empty the pots out and continue as above if that's more convenient.

Eating

In several parts of the world, canna is grown commercially for the production of starch; Vietnamese 'cellophane noodles', for instance,

Canna rhizomes, for eating or propagating

are made of canna starch. But canna is also a traditional vegetable, boiled or baked, especially in South America. I've only ever eaten the rhizomes, but in some countries the young leaf shoots are used as a vegetable and the large leaves as wraps.

I use canna rather unimaginatively as a bulk 'root' crop for casseroles, stews, and thick soups, where it behaves very much like a potato. It doesn't have a strong flavour, being slightly sweet, mildly potatoey. It's probably fair to say that it's useful – unobtrusively pleasant – rather than exciting. It's at its most useful at that time of the winter when the potatoes in the shops have developed a glassy texture and a nasty, sweet taste.

The rhizomes are simply prepared by washing, dicing and boiling. Canna does need a longer cooking time than most root or tuber vegetables, however, as even at its least fibrous, it is still rather fibrous. Just to warn you: the flesh becomes mucilaginous and translucent when cooked, which is nicer than it sounds. Nutritionists consider it to be unusually easy to digest, so it's often recommended as a food for invalids and convalescents. It can be eaten raw, though I must admit I've never quite felt up to the challenge.

Mallow (*Malva*) flower

Mallow (*Malva sylvestris*)

Also known as: Common mallow, High mallow, Country mallow, Wood mallow, Cheeses, Cheese flower.

In very hot countries *Malva* is an annual; in the Mediterranean it's a biennial; and in Britain it's a short-lived perennial, best replaced about every three years. However, it often self-seeds, so a clump may renew itself without any intervention from the gardener. As far back as history goes, it's been used for food in many parts of the world, including Britain, though it's best known now as a cottage garden flower.

Ornamental value

Malva produces lots of pink or purple flowers, an inch or two across, from early summer to early autumn, which are attractive to bees. Its crinkly, quite fleshy, ivy-shaped leaves remain green pretty well all year round, even during frosty weather. The plant reaches 18-36 inches (46-91 cm) tall (though it can get much taller in shade), with a spread of around 18 inches (46 cm). It is a fast growing plant, flowering and reaching full height even in its first year from seed. Cultivars specially bred for their flowers are available, and are also edible.

How to start

Sow seeds in pots, tray or modules in April or May, preferably under cover. Mallow seeds germinate quickly, sometimes in a few days and usually within the month, though they can be erratic so don't give up on them too soon. You can also sow them in their final position, in late summer, for the following year.

In spring and early summer, you can buy *Malva* in pots for planting out, or you can take basal cuttings from existing plants. Look for a new shoot growing from the base of the clump. With a sharp knife or secateurs, cut it off at the point where it joins the older, woodier part of the plant. Remove all its lower leaves, so it still has its hairdo, but the stem is bare. Look for a slight bump on the stem – this is a leaf node. Make a straight cut just below that, so that you're left with a cutting that's about 4 inches (10 cm) long.

If there's a growing tip, pinch that off with your fingers. Immediately plant the cutting in the smallest pot it will fit into, in a potting mixture that is very well-drained; I use half peat-free multipurpose compost (by volume) mixed with half horticultural grit (which is sold at garden centres and DIY stores). Poke the stem into the compost at the edge of the pot, so that its leaves are only just clear

Mallow (*Malva*) seedling

of the surface. Put the pot into a sealed plastic bag to retain humidity, and place it somewhere out of direct sun, but still in good light, at ordinary room temperature or in a greenhouse. The compost needs to be kept moist, but mustn't become wet. If the inside surface of the bag is dripping, or water is pooling beneath the pot, that counts as wet. After a few weeks, roots should have formed. With luck, you'll be able to see them poking out of the drainage holes of the pot. If not, give the cutting a gentle tug – if you feel resistance, you've probably got roots. Remove the bag once you're confident the cutting has rooted.

GROWING

When seedlings are around 4 inches (10 cm) tall, probably in late spring or early summer, plant them out 12-18 inches (30-46 cm) apart. Bought plants, or those grown from cuttings, should be planted out after the last frost, when they're well-established and putting on new growth.

Malva will grow in most places, but it does get leggy in shade, and is best in full sun. The soil should be well-drained, but only moderately fertile. Don't site malva in your richest or poorest piece of ground. Never feed this plant unless it's struggling; it doesn't prosper on an overly nitrogenous diet. Water during dry weather.

The leaves become tougher – and therefore less pleasant to eat – as the plant flowers. You could keep cutting the plants back to prevent, or at least delay, flowering. You can also cut individual stalks back after they've flowered to encourage new growth. There's no need to cut dead stalks off in autumn, unless you want to for the sake of tidiness.

Malva does all right in a large container, but only if you can keep it sufficiently watered in high summer. It wilts alarmingly in hot weather, and needs soaking at least twice a day. It's unlikely that these dramatic swoons will be fatal, assuming you're able to water the tub every few days, but they do look a bit off-putting.

PROBLEMS

I've never had any problem with pests on *Malva*, but it's commonly affected by rust, a fungal condition. If you can get hold of some comfrey fertiliser, home-made or bottled, give rusty plants a good drenching all through the summer, weekly, and that will often get rid of it.

In windy positions, or if they get very tall, *Malva* plants might need staking – I have had them topple over.

HARVEST & STORAGE

Spring is the best time for harvesting the leaves, when they're young and plentiful, but I've taken them in smaller quantities during the other three seasons as well. They will keep in a plastic bag in the fridge for a day or so. The foliage is best cut with scissors, so that you can remove the leaves from the stems, the latter tending towards hairiness. Also in spring, the tender tips of new growth can be steamed as a vegetable.

The seed capsules, the so-called 'cheeses' or 'nuts', are best when they're immature; look for a light green colour and a texture that's crisp rather than hard.

EATING

The leaves of common mallow have a mild flavour – some might say bland – and an agreeable soft texture. It's a very easy thing to eat, if you know what I mean. It will neither offend nor excite the fussiest palate, or the most troubled digestion.

It's precisely this mildness which makes mallow such a useful plant to have in your garden, because it can be used in considerable bulk, often alongside stronger tasting greens. The young leaves, for instance, will play the lettuce role of making up the mass of a salad, which is then enlivened with tangier items.

At any age, the mucilaginous leaves make a good thickener for soups. Steamed or boiled until tender, which should take no longer than four or five minutes, they will substitute for spinach. They can be sautéed in oil as a side vegetable or used in place of vine leaves for dolmades, and are excellent in risotto. Mallow petals are used in salad as an edible decoration.

Some readers will remember from childhood the disappointment of discovering that mallow 'cheeses' didn't taste like cheese, any more than hawthorn's 'bread-and-cheese leaves' tasted of bread and cheese. Or of anything. The fruits of common *Malva* are all right, though; they have a crunch to them, and a slightly sweet flavour. They're usually eaten just as they are – 'eaten from hand' as the fruit breeders say – though I have heard of them being fermented.

As for the name, it's true that mallow cheeses do look a bit like tiny wheels of cheese. But what they also look a bit like is...well, you know when you find a small, lime-green caterpillar curled up in your salad, but someone else is kindly paying for the meal so you don't like to make a fuss? Mallow cheeses look a bit like that.

Flower spike of amaranth (*Amaranthus*)

Amaranth (*Amaranthus*)

Also known as: Love-lies-bleeding, Callaloo, Pigweed,
Kiwicha, Prince's feather, Elephant head.

Historically used as a food on almost every continent – and still quite widely used today – amaranth was one of the most important crops of the Aztecs until they were conquered by the Spanish. One of the Aztec uses for amaranth grain was to mix it with honey and form it into religious figures. Consequently their new Christian masters banned cultivation of the plant, and so one of the world's most useful foods became obscure and ended up as a mere ornamental. Amaranth has never regained its former eminence, although modern nutritionists are very keen on it, believing that its particular combination of proteins makes it a near-perfect food for the human digestive system. As well as being high in protein, it is also gluten-free, which has brought it some recent attention.

There are scores of species in the genus *Amaranthus*, several of which grow easily and well in Britain. Indeed, some are self-seeding weeds. The amaranth most commonly seen in our parks and gardens is love-lies-bleeding (*A. caudatus*) which, as luck would have it, is also the species most often recommended for grain production. (Technically they're seeds, not grain, but they are used as grain.) It's not frost hardy, and is grown in this country as an annual. According to Garden Organic (formerly the Henry Doubleday Research Association), 'All the many members of the genus *Amaranthus* are edible, although some are better than others.'

I'm writing here about growing amaranth for grain, but its spinachy leaves are also widely eaten, often under the name 'callaloo'. My feeling is that callaloo is more of a back garden vegetable, less suitable for an invisible allotment, because you'll want to delay its flowering as long as possible so as to get more foliage.

Ornamental value

This is an unusual case where the types sold for vegetables tend to be even more colourful than the ones sold as ornamentals. Having said that, all amaranths are beautiful plants. Their large leaves, looking something like giant basil, can be red, green, yellow or multi-coloured. Even the stems are colourful. But the flower tassels which appear in summer, made up of masses of tiny blooms like bunches of huge catkins, are the main point of ornamental interest. Depending on the species, variety, or cultivar you're growing, you might get red, pink, yellow, gold or purple flowers; there are even some cultivars in pale green or a kind of yellowish white. Mixed packets of seed intended either for grain or leaf production are available, which will give a delightful range of colours.

There's also a great variation in the size of the plants themselves, and the shape and arrangement of their tassels. I've had amaranths a foot tall (30 cm), 5 feet tall (1.5 metres), and all stops in between – and I know there are some which will grow shorter or taller than that. They all seem to produce decent amounts of seed, no matter what their height. The flower tassels are sometimes upright, sometimes hanging, some form in tufts, and some are two feet long. There's an amaranth called 'Dreadlocks', a name which gives a good mental image of its flowers.

How to start

Seed of love-lies-bleeding is sold by most seed catalogues, a few of which also list amaranth as a vegetable. I sow the seeds around May Day each year in a small seed tray, indoors on a bright windowsill. Amaranth germinates quickly at a temperature of about 60 °F (15.5 °C), and within a fortnight I'll be pricking out the crowded seedlings into individual small pots or cellular trays in my unheated greenhouse. Slightly less dependably, but much more simply, try sprinkling some seed over a patch of soil in May, when the ground is warm and moist, and lightly raking it in.

You can sometimes buy love-lies-bleeding plants in garden centres in spring.

Growing

The plants are ready to go outside once they are about 6 inches (15 cm) tall, and the last frost has been and gone. I aim to get mine out somewhere about the 10th of June – depending, obviously, on soil and weather conditions. Even in a cool summer, amaranth is an impressively and gratifyingly fast-growing plant.

Amaranths must have a position in full sun, and they must have good drainage. Other than that, they are famously adaptable. For one thing, they're drought tolerant, which incidentally makes them good subjects for growing in containers; the pots still need to be quite large, say 30 or 40 litres, because in anything smaller the tall plants are likely to topple over in the wind. Even in the open ground it can be necessary to stake them against wind. I've seen some of the smaller types grown in window boxes, which looks dramatic and would presumably give the plant extra heat from the house.

If you've got the choice, plant your amaranths in an open-textured soil, rather than a heavy one, and avoid very rich ground. Never feed them.

If you're planting a few, then a spacing of 20 inches (51 cm) is about right; I've grown them at spaces of 1 foot, 18 inches and 2 feet (30 cm, 46 cm, and 61 cm) without noticing much difference in performance. Really, you can just stick them randomly into any sunny gap – despite being potentially big plants, their footprint is not large, and most of the action happens up top. To an extent, they adapt their growth to how much space you give them. If you're confident of a hot summer (I'm not sure how you would be, but if you are…) you could try putting them a yard (1 metre) apart. With luck you'll get really spectacular plants and a big harvest of seeds.

Water them in with a full watering can each after planting.

PROBLEMS

I've never heard of any pests or diseases striking amaranths in this country. I'm not saying there *aren't* any, because you know what life's like, but the only problem I've ever encountered is when I've left it too late to stake the top-heavy plants and they've gone over in a storm.

HARVEST & STORAGE

From late summer onwards, periodically check the flower tassels, either by running them through your hands or by picking one and stripping it as if you were processing it for drying (see below). If the tiny, shiny, pale round seeds – a little bigger than poppy seeds – spill freely when you do that, then it's harvest time. (If the flowers are scratchy and dry, and there aren't many seeds, then you've left it too late this year – in which case, just leave the plants in the ground for

Young amaranth (*Amaranthus*)

as long as they're still good to look at. Birds will eat the seeds, and the plants might self-seed for next year.)

I use secateurs to cut off all the bunches of flowers, and then, holding each tassel at the tip and running my other hand down its length, strip all the flowers into a bucket. (I almost wrote 'clean bucket' there, but really, there is a point where instructive precision tumbles into the insultingly obvious, don't you think?) Now rub the flower heads through a sieve or riddle into another bucket. (Yes, this is a two-bucket job. You may need to borrow one from your next-door neighbour. If you think it's clean enough.) The seeds will pass through the sieve, while the flowers and bits of plant will stay in the sieve. If you get a lot of non-seed material coming through, you may be rubbing too hard, or you may need a sieve with smaller holes.

It's worth doing the sieving two or three times, as long as there's still a good amount of seed coming through. Once there are none left, or rather hardly any, give up – you'll never get every single seed out, and you could go mad trying. Anyway, in a good year there will be thousands of seeds per plant. Discard everything other than the seeds into the compost bin. Spread the seeds on a shallow tray under cover for a couple of days to dry slightly.

Sorry – something I should have mentioned earlier: some ripe seeds will spill at every stage of harvesting and processing, so it's a good idea to spread some newspaper around to catch them.

Depending on how well the business with the buckets went, you may want to winnow the seed to get rid of the chaff, that is the bits of plant that are still mixed in with the grain. This is much easier than it sounds, and much more exciting, too. Pick a dry day, ideally one where there is a gentle breeze coming consistently from one direction. Put your amaranth seeds into a container like a big saucepan, and take them outside. Pour the seeds smoothly, through

EAT YOUR FRONT GARDEN

Amaranth (*Amaranthus*) flowers ready for sieving

the air, from one container to another. They tend to bounce when they land, so I put a cloth at the bottom of the bucket to deaden their momentum.

The chaff is lighter than the grain, so in the right breeze, at the right angle, it'll flow away in a stream while the heavier seeds fall into the second container. Winnowing isn't so much a skill as an attitude: it works much better if you handle it confidently and boldly, as if you've been doing it since you were knee-high, and couldn't be less worried about messing it up. The first time you get it right you'll probably have to supress a yell of triumph, several fist pumps, and possibly a few jig steps. Repeat the winnowing a few times, if necessary, until all you've got left is clean grain. Now spread the grain out again, as before, to dry thoroughly, before storing it in an airtight container in a cool, dark cupboard, where it will last for months.

EATING

Amaranth grain has a good, nutty flavour, and it's surprisingly filling – you don't need much. It's also a versatile food, served in a variety of ways in both sweet and savoury dishes.

There are three main methods of cooking the dried seed. You can simply add it as it is to recipes such as soups, stews, casseroles and so on, to make them heartier. Whenever you're using rice, add some amaranth to it while it's cooking to make it tastier, more nutritious and generally more interesting.

Or you can cook amaranth on its own in a pan of water, as if it were rice. Don't overcook it or it'll get soggy – twenty minutes should be plenty. Then you can use it as it is, hot or cold.

Finally – and this is my favourite method – you can pop amaranth seeds. Get a heavy-bottomed pan, the sort that will take a high flame without sticking or burning. Heat it – without adding any oil, butter, water or anything else – until it's reached a temperature where, if you dropped water into it, the water would immediately evaporate. If you're familiar with cooking with a wok, you'll know the temperature I'm talking about – it's when the wok begins to smoke. Add the dried amaranth grains a spoonful at a time, and stir them around, gently and constantly, with a spatula. If the heat's right, they will instantly start popping. You'll see the whiteness appearing, just as with popcorn, as their hulls burst and turn inside out. They'll also double in size, though since they're so tiny to start with that isn't easy to spot. When the popping noise stops, tip the amaranth out into a bowl and replace it with the next batch. (I've tried popping amaranth in a popcorn maker, but without success; perhaps amaranth needs a higher temperature than corn.)

Popped amaranth is excellent eaten as a more flavoursome alternative to popcorn, but you can also use it as a breakfast cereal, or as a slightly crunchy topping on any sweet or savoury dish where you might otherwise put crumble or breadcrumbs. It would also be very good, say, as part of a salad in a lunchbox (though I think it's important to add that if you're under pressure to eat your lunch at your workstation, then you should join a trade union – all humans are entitled to a proper lunch break).

I'm sure you'll find other ways of cooking and using amaranth if you experiment with it. In some parts of the Americas, it's made into cakes and confectionary, or ground into flour. The possibilities can't literally be endless, I suppose, but they're certainly numerous.

Garlic chives (*Allium tuberosum*) in bloom

GARLIC CHIVES (*ALLIUM TUBEROSUM*)

Also known as: Chinese chives, Jiu cai, Gow (or Gao) choy,
Chinese leek, Nira, Oriental garlic, Flowering chives, Flat
chives, Golden chives.

Chives themselves don't get into this book, despite being edible
and ornamental, because really we only ever use them as a
garnish, and because they look like what they are: edible herbs.
Garlic chives, though, are a different matter. Popular in much
of Asia, particularly in China, garlic chives are (or 'is', I can
never decide) a significant vegetable crop. That's especially true
of the stems with flower buds on, widely sold in bunches as a
premium item in markets. This is a perennial plant, very hardy,
unlikely to be killed by high or low temperatures, which grows
as a slowly expanding, flat clump, spread by rhizomes, and can
easily live for ten or twenty years.

ORNAMENTAL VALUE

The small, white, star-like flowers which appear in late summer,
arranged in dome-shaped sprays, on stems around 15-18 inches (38-
46 cm) tall, really are strikingly lovely, worthy of a place in any rock
garden or bed devoted to flowering bulbs. Garlic chives is a much
more impressive ornamental than many ornamentals.

Months before flowering, the first bright green new leaves
emerge very early in spring. They'll grow to be about a foot

(30 cm) high, and half an inch (12 mm) wide. These are flat, solid leaves, not tubular like those of chives (or, indeed, onions). Garlic chives is a compact, neat grower – much more so than chives – with drooping foliage, which dies back (sometimes completely, sometimes just mostly) during winter. The flowers will be covered with hoverflies and bees in late summer and early autumn.

HOW TO START

The best way is to divide an existing clump in spring or autumn. If you don't know anyone who's already got garlic chives, then you can buy them in small pots from many nurseries or online plant suppliers. The cheapest way, of course, is to buy a packet of seed, available from most seed companies.

Seeds are usually sown in small pots or modular trays, for planting out later. They can be sown directly into the soil, but success is much less certain. In spring or early summer, sow the seeds about half an inch (12 mm) deep in seed compost or peat-free multipurpose compost. These seeds don't remain viable for very long, so it's best to start with a fresh packet each time. Unless you're starting very early in the year they won't normally need any extra heat; a windowsill or greenhouse will do in spring, and outdoors on a patio or step should work in early summer. Be warned, though, that they can be slow to germinate. I sow roughly ten seeds in a pot or cell, later planting the whole lot out together as one clump.

In China, different varieties of garlic chives are available, particularly for either leaf or tender flower stem production. At the time of writing this, we don't have the same choice in Britain – they are usually sold simply as 'garlic chives'.

GROWING

When planting the young plants out, make sure an inch or so (2.5 cm) of the bottom of the leaves is below soil level. The lighter coloured base of the leaves, naturally blanched, is considered the tenderest and tastiest part.

Garlic chives will grow well enough in any soil, provided it's never waterlogged, and in full sun or partial shade. A rich, open soil in a sunny position, however, will probably produce the best overall growth. I find they flower more in sun, and produce edible leaf for longer in some shade. They're fairly resistant to drought, so can be useful for filling any dry spots in the garden.

Spacing isn't very important – just put the clumps in wherever you want them. But if you are planning to grow a number of plants together, in a formal bed or as a border alongside a path for instance, place them about 14 inches (35.5 cm) apart.

Once they're established, there's very little for you to do. Mulch the plants with a couple of inches of thoroughly rotted garden compost every spring, and if they look as if they need it, give them a general purpose feed, such as a proprietary seaweed liquid, after taking a harvest three or four times a year. If they seem to be thriving, then just leave them alone – plants don't need cossetting except when they do.

If the clump gets too big for your purposes or begins to look a bit cramped and overcrowded, dig it up with a garden fork in spring or autumn, pull it apart into smaller portions, and replant the surplus elsewhere or donate it to a neighbour. Give the remainder another mulch of compost, a good watering, and a firming with your boot to settle it back in. They don't need regular division, the way chives do, even when container grown, but if you feel that after a few years their vigour has declined, or the individual leaves are becoming smaller, try splitting the clump.

Unless you want to produce seed for resowing, don't let the flowers go to seed. Cut them off as they begin to turn old, to encourage further growth. (Having said this, the dried heads left on the plants can be quite ornamental in a winter frost.)

In China, garlic chives are often 'blanched', producing yellow leaves which have a noticeably milder, sweeter flavour. These are known as 'golden chives'. Blanching, in this sense, means covering a cut-back plant so that the next flush of growth comes up in darkness. This can be achieved by drawing soil up over the plant, or by covering it with a terracotta blanching pot, or an ordinary flower pot that's had the hole in the base sealed with heavy-duty masking tape, or by using a large plastic bucket or a solid box. If you know how to blanch rhubarb, sea kale or chicory, you can use the same techniques and equipment on garlic chives. Blanching weakens a plant, but shouldn't kill it, so only blanch any individual clump once per year and then let it recover.

Garlic chives is very easily grown in containers, especially large, wide tubs, but anything larger than an 8 inch (20 cm) pot will do. The plants will need more attentive watering and feeding in containers. In the open ground they need watering while establishing, but after that I only ever water them if they look really distressed in midsummer.

It's probably a good idea, as with most perennials, not to crop from them during their first year so as to let them get established.

Problems

Garlic chives are as easy to grow as chives. Which is pretty easy. They need good weeding, but the mulch will help with that. I've never seen them attacked by slugs, snails or birds, even when the plants are

Leaves of garlic chives (*Allium tuberosum*) ready for cooking

very young. In fact, the only pest I've ever known on garlic chives was at the end of one hot summer, when a clump I was growing in a tub was suddenly and totally covered with blackflies, so that from a distance the whole clump looked black. I think the plants were vulnerable because I'd forgotten to water them. In any case, they recovered perfectly well over winter.

Like most edible alliums, garlic chives can suffer from a fungal disease called rust. You'll know it from the orange pustules on the leaves. The only thing to do is to get rid of all the rusty foliage as soon as possible – again, the plants will usually recover over winter.

The roots in a clump have a tendency to rise to the surface over time. Just add a couple of inches more soil or compost to cover them again.

Harvest & Storage

The leaves are ready to be harvested once they're 6 inches (15 cm) tall, and can be cut at or just below soil level two or three times in a season. Or just take a few leaves at a time, as and when you need them. If you want flowers (and you definitely do in this case) leave some areas of foliage uncut.

Connoisseurs of garlic chives tend to harvest the leaves in spring and then leave them to grow during the summer. In early autumn, they'll cut the plants down to the ground, to give another flush of fresh growth. Certainly the leaves aren't at their best for eating during summer – a bit tough and with a slightly coarsened flavour – but lacking a refined palate, I use them anyway.

The closed flower buds can be taken on their own, or still attached to their stalks. Flowers in bloom are cut from the stalks, which will by now be too tough for eating.

Cut garlic chives will store in the fridge in a plastic bag for a few days, maybe up to a week. Golden chives will only last a day or two. The leaves can be stored for winter use, either dried or frozen, but they are available fresh for so long that I rarely bother.

Eating

I don't think there's any plant in my garden that gets eaten on as many days of the year as garlic chives does. Whatever you're having for lunch, unless it's cornflakes, a few snips of garlic chives is bound to improve it – a sandwich, a soup, a potato, an egg or some cheese. Add them to a pot of instant noodles and you will come to believe that the little plastic tubs must have co-evolved alongside garlic chives, since they so obviously belong together.

Whereas chives have a mild onion flavour, garlic chives have a mild garlic flavour. They are more substantial than chives and will stand up to cooking better. 'Flowering chives', that is the stems with flower buds on them, are usually cut into one inch (2.5 cm) pieces and added to recipes such as stir-fries, noodle dishes and soups, during the last few minutes of cooking. Flowers in bloom are used in the same way, having first been broken into florets, and are especially good raw in salads or scattered across cooked dishes.

Unlike chives, garlic chives are frequently used in some bulk – a whole supermarket bunch might go into one dish. I've seen Chinese recipes to serve four people which use half a pound of flowering chives as the main vegetable in a meat dish.

The leaves are often included in dumplings, or tied in bundles and deep-fried in batter as a side dish. Golden chives can be used in the same way as the ordinary leaves, but perhaps to make best use of their delicate flavour, impressive colour and luxurious rarity, they should be served separately as appetisers. There are times in the lives of those who grow their own vegetables when ostentation is the only reasonable approach.

Sunflower (*Helianthus*)

SUNFLOWER (*HELIANTHUS ANNUUS*)

Also known as: Common sunflower.

This familiar hardy annual is a major global crop for its edible seeds and especially for the oil that's made from them. But I'm not suggesting growing it for its seeds here – they're worth a go if you're keen, but I find them fiddly and unreliable in our climate. Besides, there is an actual, bona fide vegetable hidden in the sunflower which I'll describe below.

Various other parts of the plant are used for an impressive range of commercial purposes, including cloth-making, and the sunflower is also raised commercially as a cut flower and a garden ornamental. It's useful to wildlife, especially insects and birds.

ORNAMENTAL VALUE

Sunflowers have long been grown in front gardens for their big, cheerful, sun-shaped flower heads, made up of many tiny flowers, which bloom in summer from a spring sowing. The many cultivars of sunflower range from about a foot (30 cm) high, to those specimens 16 feet (5 m) tall that schoolchildren grow to win local newspaper competitions. Some have single heads on a single stem, while others are branching and multi-headed. All are edible.

HOW TO START

Because I grow sunflowers primarily for the edible flower

buds, I prefer varieties that have lots of heads. If you're more interested in eating the seeds, then you want a sunflower with a single, very big head. Those bred for their seeds to be eaten, rather than made into oil, usually have striped seeds, and are known in the trade as 'confection sunflowers'. Any cultivar that has F1 in the name is likely to produce no seed, or else barren seed. Some seed catalogues will give suggestions as to which sunflower is best for which use. If you're not too bothered either way, then just go by the picture on the seed packet or on the nurseryman's website to choose the colour and height that you prefer.

In spring, sunflowers are available as plug plants from garden centres and online, or you can raise your own plants from seed. Sow the seeds half an inch (12 mm) deep, either in the open ground where you want them to grow, from the start of May, or singly in 3 ½ inch (9 cm) pots in seed compost, indoors at room temperature during March and April, keeping them in good light all the time so they don't develop long, bendy stems.

GROWING

Plant out sunflowers in early May. They're not very big plants at ground level, so they don't need a lot of space – about 18 inches (46 cm) between sunflowers, or between a sunflower and another neighbouring plant, should be enough. They'll grow to some extent in most conditions, but they're better in a sunny position, in deep, rich soil. Sunflowers take quite a lot out of the soil, so for the benefit of the next plant remember to give the ground plenty of manure or compost after the crop is finished. They are quite drought tolerant once established, but keep them well-watered for plenty of good growth. They

Shield bug on sunflower (*Helianthus*) seed head

don't really need feeding, unless you actually have entered a tallest sunflower competition, in which case you do realise you're going to break a lot of children's hearts when you walk off with their prize?

Depending on how tidy you feel the need to be in your front garden, at the end of the season, in autumn, you might like to leave any remaining dead flower heads for the birds to feed on over the winter. Dead stalks are also useful for insects to hide in. If you can't do that, cut the stalks and heads down and kick them somewhere out of the way, perhaps under a hedge, where the wildlife will find them anyway. Note that if left alone in autumn, sunflowers will often self-sow for new plants next spring.

Problems

If the sunflowers you've sown don't come up at all, it's quite possible they were eaten by mice who will go to some lengths to get hold of these extraordinarily nutritious seeds. Slugs will attack the very young plants; to avoid this, pot the plants on progressively until they're about a foot tall before planting them out. Fully grown sunflowers are strong, sturdy plants, but even so I've known them to come down in gales, so consider staking them if your garden is a windy one.

Harvest & Storage

To harvest sunflower buds – sometimes called sunflower 'artichokes' – look for flower heads that haven't yet opened into flowers, from midsummer onwards. Some people prefer them when they're still completely green, and some when the first signs of yellow petals are visible. The nearer they are to flowering the stronger their piney flavour becomes, so pick them at various stages to find out which you prefer. Cut the bud from the plant, and pull off the green sepals at the base, which are likely to be bitter. Sunflower buds will keep for a few days in the fridge, especially in a Green Bag (see Resources, pages 234-5), but are definitely best eaten on the day of picking.

Eating

This is a remarkably edible plant. Apart from the famous seeds, the leaves can be cooked as greens (though not by me – great hairy, coarse things that they are), and the young stalks, peeled, are sometimes used as an alternative to celery. The petals are eaten in salads and rice dishes; they're colourful, but I've never found them very tasty. The big, open flower heads are eaten stuffed, like flat mushrooms.

In my opinion, though, and in my kitchen, the main course of the sunflower feast is the flower bud. Start by cutting off the remains of its stalk, and its raised base, so that the back of the bud – the part that was attached to the plant – is now flat. That can be done before or after blanching; after is messier, but before is tougher. To blanch the bud, either steam it for about five minutes or boil it for about three minutes, until it's tender enough that a sharp knife will go straight through, from back to front, without meeting resistance. (If, on eating the buds, you find them bitterer than you like, try changing the water halfway through blanching.)

Finish trimming the bud using a knife or kitchen scissors to remove the outer, tougher leaves, as if scraping the 'tyre' from the rim of the 'wheel'. What you're left with is a pale disc which looks almost exactly like a trimmed artichoke heart – it tastes much the same, too, and is frequently used in just the same ways.

You can eat the blanched, trimmed buds as they are, hot or cold, with or without melted butter and lemon juice, or salt and pepper, when their nutty, resinous, earthy flavour is at its best. But you can also sauté, grill, braise or bake them, or use them as ingredients in any number of recipes. They're very good included in any *au gratin* dish.

Bellflower (*Campanula*)

BELLFLOWER (*CAMPANULA*)

Also known as: Rampion, Rapunzel,
Bats-in-the-belfry, Harebells.

There are about 400 species in the genus *Campanula*, many of them
familiar as garden flowers. Several of them are also used for food.
There are annual, biennial and perennial members of the genus.
They'll grow easily in a wide range of conditions. The bellflowers
I've found most useful are:

* *C. versicolor*, apparently the only scented species, its blooms
smelling of cloves. It's an increasingly popular salad plant,
because its mild, easy-to-eat leaves, which taste a little like
garden peas, can be used in bulk, the way you might use
lettuce. Although it can be killed by a winter that's both
unusually cold and unusually wet, it's otherwise a reliable
perennial, growing eventually 4 feet (1.2 m) tall and 3 feet (1 m)
across. During ordinary winter weather the foliage will often
continue to grow slowly, and can be harvested moderately.

* *C. trachelium*, reputedly the best bellflower for growing on
clay soils, as well as being a good eater. It can reach 3 feet (1 m)
tall, with a spread of 12 inches (30 cm).

* *C. latifolia*, the Giant Bellflower, can grow to 6 feet (2 m)

high, and 2 feet (61 cm) across. Spectacular to look at, and with roots that are large enough to be easily used in the kitchen, it does have a reputation in some quarters for being difficult to get rid of once you've got it.

* *C. persicifolia*, the Peach-Leaved Bellflower, is one of the most popular garden campanulas, with exceptional flowers and many named cultivars to choose from. It's quick-growing, reaching 3 feet (1 m) tall by 1 foot (30 cm) wide, and suited to dappled shade, such as you find on the edge of woodland.

* *C. rapunculus*, known as rampion, was a popular root vegetable in Europe for centuries, especially in the Middle Ages. It's also one of the best ornamentals, forming neat clumps, 3 feet (1 m) tall by 1 foot (30 cm) wide, ideal for growing in large pots. It's a hardy biennial or short-lived perennial. Don't confuse it with *C. rapunculoides*, which some gardeners find spreads as a weed.

Ornamental value

Bellflowers are often sold as cottage garden plants because they look so right in a British garden. They're whatever the opposite of 'exotic looking' is, with their fairly small, unflashy green leaves and delicate flowers in blue, mauve or white, which bloom mainly from mid-summer to early autumn. Some years, I get flowers as early as June and as late as December. They mostly have bell-shaped flowers, hence both the English and Latin names, but there are some species with tubular, star, or cup-and-saucer shaped blooms. Most of the campanulas produce a good number of flowers during the season, which are attractive to bees and other pollinators.

Some are evergreen, and more are sometimes evergreen, depending on the weather; most of the rest start showing new foliage in early spring. In terms of growth, they are variously trailing, clumping, low and spreading, or upright.

How to start

Both seeds and young plants are widely available and easily grown. Because bellflowers are such popular ornamentals, you'll find a good choice (especially online) of species, forms, colours and named cultivars.

Sow the seeds indoors – in a cool room, or in a cold frame or unheated greenhouse – in March or April, or sow outdoors in May. The seeds are very fine, so get a plastic sandwich bag, put a handful of horticultural sand (see Resources, pages 234-5) into it, and then add a pinch of seed, and mix them together. That'll mean the seeds are reasonably well spread out, and they won't need covering with compost or soil. Under cover, spread the seedy sand over the surface of the compost in a 4 inch (10 cm) pot which is almost full of seed compost or peat-free multipurpose compost. When planting outside, spread the seedy sand along a very shallow 'drill' in the soil – just a line drawn with your finger, really. In both cases, take care to make sure the sand never dries out. Outside, keep the drill thoroughly weeded.

When the indoor seedlings are big enough to handle, or when the original pot is starting to look overcrowded, move each seedling on to its own small pot, in peat-free multipurpose compost. Plant them out into their permanent positions in the garden, or in tubs, when they've got strong roots and the last frost has passed. The same goes for plants which you've bought in.

You can also take basal cuttings from existing plants in spring. Find a shoot 4 inches (10 cm) long which is growing from the base of the plant, down at ground or compost level. Cut it off with a sharp knife as close to the main body of the plant as you can. Pot it up in a gritty compost and keep it indoors. In a few weeks its roots should fill the pot, and it can be planted out.

Growing

Most campanulas grow best in full sun or very light shade. Some, including rampion, don't do so well in very hot positions, where they will run to seed, producing fewer flowers and smaller roots. Any ordinarily fertile soil will do, provided it never gets waterlogged.

Especially in pots, but even in the ground, bellflowers will need watering right through the growing season.

To get the best quality roots for eating, it's usually recommended to remove the flowers. That would impair their invisibility, of course, and in any case you'll still get some roots, whether or not you de-flower the plants.

Problems

There's nothing much to worry about except slugs, and sometimes snails. In less sluggy gardens like mine, it'll usually only be the young spring growth that's affected, but if you already know that your garden is badly troubled by slugs then you should probably grow your campanulas in pots, raised off the ground on pot feet.

Harvest & Storage

Young shoots are taken in spring, young leaves (the older ones can get a bit tough) throughout the growing season, and the roots in autumn, or through the winter.

The leaves don't keep well; pick them on the day of use, if possible. The roots can be stored like other root crops – in the fridge for about a week, and in boxes of moist sand for a few weeks.

EATING

The flowers of some species are eaten in salads. If you've got an especially refined palate, you might detect a slight sweetness to them. The leaves, on the other hand, are a proper crop, cooked or raw. The flavour is mild, but far from bland, and again slightly sweet. Usually when you say of a food 'You couldn't really dislike it' you're damning it with faint praise, but in this case it means that there's nothing very striking about the taste of the leaves, they're just very palatable.

To cook them as a green vegetable, steam or boil them for a short time until they're just tender. (That also applies to the spring stems.) Steamed, dried in a teacloth, and then fried in oil and garlic, the leaves are lovely. They also make a good soup ingredient.

Several bellflowers – most famously rampion – produce taproots up to 8 inches long which are big enough to be worth eating. Even then, they're not actually *big* – they're more comparable to slender carrots – but they are definitely worth eating. First, wash them and scrape off a thin layer of their skin.

Raw, they are used like radishes, but without any heat in the taste. They're crisp and juicy, with dense, white flesh. I like them grated in a salad, where they take up the dressing very well.

The roots are cooked in much the same way as salsify or scorzonera; boil or steam for about eight minutes, then cut them into chunks and mash, roast, or bake them. They're good in soups and savoury pies. They have a noticeably nutty flavour…well, nutty and sweet anyway.

Stridolo (*Silene*) foliage

STRIDOLO
(*SILENE VULGARIS*; SOMETIMES *S. INFLATA*)

Also known as: Bladder campion, Sculpit, Maidenstears, Bubbolini.

A more-or-less evergreen, native perennial, often found on well-drained grassland and wasteland, stridolo is best known in this country as a summer wildflower under the name bladder campion. In Cyprus, Crete, and parts of Spain and Italy, it's a popular wild green, with bunches of its leaves being seen for sale in vegetable markets. In Emilia-Romagna, Italy, there's a Stridolo Festival in spring. Sometimes prone to self-seeding, stridolo is seen as a weed in parts of North America.

ORNAMENTAL VALUE

This is an appealing plant when in bloom, delicate but also very slightly comical – the sort of flower that makes people smile when they catch sight of it. From around May to August, but especially in June and July, it puts out masses of stalked, white flowers, about an inch (2.5 cm) wide, made up of five lobed petals, behind which are pink, inflated, balloon-shaped calyces. (Or bladder-shaped if you prefer, though it's hard to imagine the sort of person who would.) The nodding flowers are held on multi-branching stems.

The upright foliage, which grows to about 2 feet (61 cm) high, is fairly ornamental – or at least quite neat-looking. The light green or grey-green leaves are narrow with pointed tips. The flowers attract butterflies, and at night, when they emit a faint scent of cloves, they'll be visited by large moths.

How to start

Seeds will be listed in either the wildflower section of catalogues and websites, as Bladder Campion, or in the vegetable section as Stridolo or Sculpit. Stridolo can be sown indoors, for planting out later, any time from early spring to early autumn, and outdoors directly into the soil from late spring to late summer. For me, it works best in big pots or tubs, with a capacity of 30 litres or more, filled with peat-free multipurpose compost, which I sow in August. I sprinkle a moderate pinch of seed over the pre-watered surface and then sift (as if sifting flour) a light covering of dry compost over it. The seedlings will show in about a week.

Plants in small pots are available online, especially in spring and autumn. I've also tried propagating from cuttings, tearing side shoots off main stems and almost burying them in small pots full of sandy compost. That works, in the sense that it makes new plants, but mine have always 'bolted' – prematurely run to seed – very quickly, so they're little use as food plants. I daresay further experimentation would be worthwhile, but in the meantime, like a lot of gardeners, I tend to treat stridolo as a biennial, sowing it at the end of the summer, eating it until it flowers the following summer, and then pulling it up when it's finished blooming, and starting a new lot from seed. If all that's more labour than you can spare, an alternative is to buy a few plants, plant them in a sunny patch of the garden, and leave them to flower and self-seed as they will, taking the greens whenever they're available.

Growing

If it's in the open ground, stridolo needs well-drained soil in full sun.

EAT YOUR FRONT GARDEN

Keep it weeded, as it can be overwhelmed by large, vigorous weeds, and regularly watered during dry weather. I rarely bother thinning the plants out, unless they look badly overcrowded.

Problems

The only thing I can think of is that the roots get quite fleshy and can be hard work to remove if you've allowed stridolo to spread around the garden and then you've changed your mind.

Harvest & Storage

You can pick the leaves whenever they're there. I harvest mine right through autumn and then again from early spring. For a few weeks in early summer the edible leaves coexist with the flowers but become sparser and tougher as summer continues.

The greens will keep a day or two in the fridge, especially if they're intended for cooking rather than eating raw, but this is a vegetable best used within a few hours of harvesting.

Eating

Stridolo's complex flavour, which is delicate overall but nonetheless distinct, includes an aroma of tarragon, some spiciness as in cress, a slight bitterness reminiscent of chicory, and some of the sweetness of fresh peas. It goes very well with egg dishes, such as flans and omelettes, as well as in risottos. The young leaves are good in salads, while the older ones are used more as a flavouring. The young shoots, picked in bunches, are suitable as the main vegetable ingredient of pasta dishes, and can also be steamed, boiled, sautéed or fried. They are commonly partnered with olive oil and garlic.

Chop suey greens (*Glebionis*)

SECTION TWO

PLANTS GROWN MAINLY FOR THEIR FOLIAGE

Japanese ginger (*Zingiber*) growing in large tubs

Japanese ginger (Zingiber mioga)

Also known as: Myoga ginger, Mioga ginger, Dancing crane.

I think this might be my favourite plant in the whole book, if you don't count nasturtium, which is my favourite plant in the whole world. Japanese ginger is so simple to grow, so dependable, and yet so unusual, both as a plant and as a food – to British eyes and tastes at least. I really cannot understand why this isn't one of the best-known garden perennials in the country. It's a deciduous, herbaceous, clump-forming plant, native to Japan, Vietnam, China and Korea, and in the same genus as ginger. Occasionally used as an ornamental in the UK, it's a widely-grown food crop in Japan, where its flower buds are a common sight in supermarkets.

Ornamental value

Present from late spring or early summer until mid-autumn its lush, vibrant green, lance-shaped leaves reach about 15 inches (38 cm) in length, carried on numerous stems 3 feet (1 metre) tall. It spreads to 4-5 feet (1.2-1.5 m).

Myoga sometimes flowers in the autumn, the blooms looking like small orchids, pale yellow and fragrant.

How to start

Japanese ginger grows from rhizomes, so any time in spring either buy a new plant – several online nurseries sell it – or divide an existing clump.

A bought plant will probably arrive as a small pot with nothing obvious in it. Leave it somewhere sheltered, such as a greenhouse, bright porch or windowsill, until it is growing strongly. This could take some weeks: Japanese ginger emerges from its winter dormancy late in spring, or even early summer. Once it's up, it reaches its full height quickly.

To propagate a new plant from existing stock, I use my fingers in the soil around the old clump to locate a good-sized lump of rhizome, which I then carve off from the main body using a serrated knife or small saw. This can be quite energetic work, but at least you don't have to worry about being too rough – Japanese ginger is a tough plant that won't suffer from indelicate handling.

Plant the new division into a plastic pot big enough to take it easily, in peat-free multipurpose compost or good soil. Later in the summer, when it's growing strongly, plant it out.

Growing

Japanese ginger is a woodland plant, often found as an understory species growing beneath trees, so in this country it does best in a fairly shady position, with dappled sunlight. My main clump is near an apple tree, which suits it perfectly. It wants a rich soil, moist but well-drained.

You don't need to take any special trouble over planting Japanese ginger. Just dig a hole so that the plant will be at approximately the same depth as it was when in its pot, firm the soil around it as you refill the hole, and water it in thoroughly. If you're growing more than one plant, put them about 18 inches (46 cm) apart, bearing in mind that Japanese ginger spreads itself outwards steadily over the years.

Once the foliage is growing well, lay a mulch of garden compost, well-rotted manure, or any bought-in mulch all around the plant, a couple of inches (5 cm) deep. Keep Japanese ginger well-watered throughout the summer, and it will benefit from regular feeds with a liquid fertiliser, such as seaweed concentrate.

Accounts of Japanese ginger's hardiness differ, with most writers considering it near to fully hardy in a UK winter. There are some variegated cultivars for sale, which are said to be less hardy than the plain green ones. To be safe, I cover my plants with a thick layer of fallen leaves in November, but I doubt it's necessary.

To be absolutely certain of keeping your Japanese ginger through the winter you could plant it in a large tub so it can be moved under cover during the coldest months. It is, in any case, a very suitable species for growing in containers. In autumn, the leaves yellow and then quickly die away. If the foliage hasn't gone completely by mid-November I'll cut it down, right to the ground, so as to avoid the plant's stems getting damaged by wind.

Problems

Birds might peck at the leaves, and slugs and snails might nibble at the youngest foliage in spring, but Japanese ginger grows so rapidly that pests don't have the chance to make much impact on it. The one thing that really will damage Japanese ginger is strong wind, so be sure to plant it somewhere sheltered.

Harvest & Storage

Conical flower buds (technically, they're inflorescences) appear from beneath the soil around the base of the clump in late summer or early autumn. In my garden, they start in the last week of August

Edible buds of Japanese ginger (*Zingiber*)

or the first week of September, and they'll keep coming, a few at a time, into October.

You'll find out for yourself at which stage of their growth you like them best. I take them as soon as their tips show above ground, cutting them beneath the surface (a bit like harvesting asparagus). Left a day or so longer, until they're just starting to open, they'll reach the size of a man's thumb. Japanese ginger buds are fine looking things, coloured green, white and pinkish-red.

As for storage, they'll keep for a few days in the fridge in a plastic food bag or 'Green Bag' (see Resources, pages 234-5), but are definitely at their best when used fresh.

EATING

I like to eat 'children of myoga', as they're apparently known in Japan, just as they are, either on their own or in salads, or cooked very briefly in stir-fries. The flavour is recognisably gingery, but without ginger's heat. The texture is juicy, fresh and crunchy.

In their native lands they are variously shredded – for use in soups, tofu dishes, and salads – pickled, or used in sushi and tempura.

Unlike root ginger, this plant has inedible rhizomes. As well as the buds, the Japanese also eat the blanched spring shoots – I've never tried them, as in our relatively short British growing season I want to give my Japanese ginger as much chance as possible to concentrate its energy on producing a maximum crop of buds. I *really* love those buds.

Edible bamboo shoot (*Phyllostachys*)

Bamboo
(*Phyllostachys edulis* and *P. dulcis*)

Also known as: Moso bamboo (P. edulis),
Sweetshoot bamboo (P. dulcis).

The word bamboo refers to various species of giant grasses, with hollow, jointed stems growing from an underground, jointed rhizome. These two species are long-lived, evergreen, hardy perennials, grown in temperate areas as ornamentals, and in the tropical world as a major vegetable crop. Most (many sources say *all*) other bamboos are edible, to varying degrees and with various provisos, but these two species are specifically and widely grown for food; *edulis* means 'edible', and *dulcis* means 'sweet'. They are both very easily grown in the UK, and are two of the most attractive bamboos.

Ornamental value:

I suppose everyone in Britain knows what bamboos look like: tall, grassy, animated in a breeze. For generations, they have been much loved for their elegance, and much mocked as a cliché of the suburban front garden. In this book, let it be clearly said, we sneer at the sneerers and celebrate the clichés.

How to start

Seed is rarely available, and propagation by dividing an existing stand in mid-spring, or by rhizome cuttings in early spring, is notoriously unreliable – for reasons that aren't well understood. Most people, therefore, start by buying a young plant in a pot, anytime in spring, from a nursery or from one of many specialist online suppliers.

GROWING

When your plant arrives, dig a hole in the ground and mix the soil that comes out of it with a couple of bucketfuls of compost or manure. The hole should be slightly deeper than the pot the bamboo came in, so that the top of the rootball will be an inch (2.5 cm) or so lower than the lip of the hole. Refill the hole firmly but carefully, as it's possible to damage the young shoots if you put the boot in too enthusiastically. Water thoroughly all around the plant.

Light shade is often recommended for siting bamboos, but in my garden they've done better in full sun. They'll do well enough in either, however. Give them some space if you can, so that when first planted they're a yard (1 m) or more away from anything else. They respond well to regular watering in dry weather, and from a nitrogen-rich feed every ten days or so from spring to autumn. Mulch them in autumn with old compost, to a depth of several inches, and again when the shoots appear in spring.

However, let me reassure you that if you don't do any of the above – if you plant it in the wrong position, squeezed in among other plants, forget to water it, and never feed or mulch it – bamboo will still survive and grow and look good. The above advice describes the method for getting the best out of bamboo as a food crop. What's really important (and I learned this the hard way) is that exposure to strong winds severely reduces growth. Bamboo needs a reasonably sheltered spot.

Let your new plant settle in for its first year, and perhaps longer; don't begin harvesting the shoots until the first spring in which you see a lot of them, and it seems clear that you need to cut them in order to stop the clump spreading too much. Taking too many too early could reduce the plant's vigour. Once bamboo is established it grows taller very quickly – often inches a day during spring – and should carry on doing so for decades. There are no pruning rules as such for bamboo; if any part of it offends your eye, you can cut it off whenever you get round to it.

PROBLEMS

I've never seen any pests or diseases on bamboo in this country, but there is one potential problem that everyone's heard of. Where I lived as a child there was an abandoned house nearby, the garden of which had been entirely taken over by bamboo over decades. Local kids were delighted to have their own jungle to play in, especially since it was so dense as to be entirely inaccessible to adults. I doubt the developers were so pleased years later when they started trying to clear the land for new housing. If bamboo does get away from you, it can be very hard to eradicate.

Bamboo *can* take over, but it usually doesn't. Some people go to the lengths of building barriers, a foot (30 cm) or so deep into the ground, and 3 or 4 inches (7.5-10 cm) above it, to keep the rhizomes imprisoned. But if you're eating all the new shoots, spreading is unlikely to be a problem anyway, as a shoot that's been cut off won't regrow. In other words: harvest them even when you're not eating them.

HARVEST & STORAGE

In spring, new shoots appear at ground level. Take them when they're about 4-8 inches (10-20 cm) high. The best part of the shoot is still underground, so cut them as far down as you're able – though if you're in a hurry you can just break them off at soil level by bashing them with your fist or boot. Once they're 10 or 12 inches (25-30.5 cm) tall they're likely to be too tough to be worth bothering with, but this does vary with species and cultivation, so experiment with yours to find the cut-off point.

Spring is the main cropping season, but in good conditions you should continue to get a few more through the summer.

Bamboo shoots will keep in the fridge for a day or two but are best used quickly. If you have a glut, they can be dehydrated or pickled for later use.

EATING

The preparation of bamboo shoots is harder to describe than to do. The thing to keep in mind is that the edible bit inside is pale, tender, and revealed by cutting the shoot in half lengthways, while the outer wrappings – tougher and darker – are to be discarded.

Some experts say that bamboo is not safe to eat raw, because it contains bitter compounds (rendered harmless by boiling) to deter herbivores; others insist this applies to some species, and not others. My cautious conclusion is to grow only *P. edulis* and *P. dulcis*, which are renowned for having little if any bitterness. Also, I begin by boiling the shoots in salted water for five to ten minutes, until they have no trace of bitterness. If they're still bitter, they're not ready to eat.

To British people, the most familiar way of eating bamboo shoots is of course fried or stir-fried in Chinese recipes, whole, sliced or chopped. But they can also be used in any dish, of any cuisine, that might benefit from the addition of a crunchy vegetable – soups, stews, salads, pies, anything. Fresh bamboo has much more flavour than the tinned version which we're more used to in this country. Its taste is sometimes compared to courgettes and sometimes to oysters, which isn't actually untrue, but is of no actual help – it's the texture, still crisp after cooking, which is really the point.

Perilla growing in 12 inch pot

Perilla (*Perilla frutescens*)

Also known as: Shiso, Beefsteak plant.

A bushy herb of Asian origin, treated as a tender or half-hardy annual in this country, perilla has long been familiar in Britain as an ornamental bedding plant, but is grown for food in Japan and Korea.

Ornamental value

Fast-growing, with square stems and lots of leaves, perilla looks something like *Coleus*, or perhaps a bit like a very colourful stinging nettle or a giant mint. The Victorians were keen on it for their bedding schemes, and you still see it used that way today. It's also prized as a foliage element in flower arrangements.

It comes in two main colours, deep purple or lime green, though sometimes a bicolour or variegated form is available. It can grow 2 or 3 feet (61 cm to 1 m) high and wide, or can have its growing points pinched out regularly to make a bushier plant at around 8-12 inches (20-30 cm) tall. The leaves get to about 3 inches (7.5 cm) long. In late summer perilla produces lots of flowers, but they're what gardeners call 'insignificant', meaning that if you're over fifty you won't be able to see them without your glasses on.

How to start

I feel obliged to confess that in this section I am recommending

Perilla seeds sown under home-made mini-cloche

a species which I find almost impossible to grow. I've probably had two or three successes with perilla in about twenty years of trying. The reason I'm still including it in this book is because many people find it as easy to grow as basil, and I'm hoping you'll be one of them.

If you turn out to be part of the large subset of gardeners who discover that perilla is hard to germinate, but straightforward to grow once it's germinated, then you can start by buying young plants, which are usually available online in June.

Otherwise, begin every year with fresh seed; older perilla seeds don't have a very good germination rate. Fill a small pot or small tray with moist seed compost and press about half a dozen seeds lightly into the surface of the compost – not enough to bury them, but to ensure they are fully in contact with the compost. Do this indoors any time in late spring or early summer, and if possible keep the pot in a temperature of around 68 °F (20 °C). Germination will happen (if it's going to happen at all) within about ten days, especially if you're using a heated propagator.

Two techniques which can increase the chance of germination are covering the pot with the sawn-off top of a plastic bottle, which acts as a mini-cloche and encourages humidity, and/or soaking the seeds in water for 24 hours before sowing, to break their dormancy.

When the seedlings are large enough to handle confidently, and before they become leggy from overcrowding, prick out each one into a 3.5 inch (9 cm) pot. Keep them in a light position until it's time to plant them out.

Some gardeners find perilla so easy to germinate that they broadcast the seed, just sprinkling it where they want it to grow in early to mid-summer. However, direct-sown plants aren't likely to get as big as those started off inside.

GROWING

Once you're as sure as you can be that spring has given way to summer, so that not only are there no more frosts coming, but also the nights are no longer cold, plant your young perilla at 12-15 inches (30-40 cm) apart each way. You can either put them in a container of the same sort of size, full of peat-free multipurpose compost, or plant them in the ground in a sunny spot. They prefer moist but free-draining soil: perilla won't grow so well in drought or if its roots stay wet. Plenty of organic matter forked into the soil, such as compost or manure, will help. Perilla will grow in poor soils, but less enthusiastically. For the very best quality of foliage, mulch the surface around the plants with compost or leafmould.

Problems

I've never seen any pests or diseases on perilla. This herb is thought to be injurious to cattle, and perhaps other livestock – so, you know, if you keep a cow in your front garden don't let her eat the perilla.

Harvest & Storage

Cut off individual leaves as required throughout the summer, once the plant is growing strongly. The leaves nearest the tip tend to be the tenderest. Fresh leaves won't keep very long – maybe a day or two in a bag in the fridge – but perilla dries or freezes well for winter use.

Perilla flowers in late summer and is killed by the first frosts of autumn (if it's still alive by then). The plants will sometimes deteriorate, suddenly and dramatically, at the end of summer, the leaves going brown. When that happens, you might as well pull the plants up: they're finished, and the flavour has gone.

Eating

Aromatic, and with a flavour in which different eaters detect different tastes – including basil, cumin, anise, tangy fruit, and mint – torn-up perilla leaves are excellent as a flavouring herb for dishes containing rice, pasta, potatoes or eggs. They're used sparingly in salads, because of the strong flavour, and less cautiously in soups and stews.

The leaves can also be substituted for basil, mint or parsley – as a garnish, for instance, or in making a pesto. Perilla leaves work with sweet dishes too, such as scattered over ice cream.

Red leaves give a pink colouring to food, and are often used for that purpose in Japan in pickles, especially of plums and sliced ginger. The Japanese also use whole leaves as a wrapping for sushi, or steamed as a green vegetable, particularly to accompany oily food, or fried in batter as tempura.

Tea, hot or iced, can be made from the leaves. In general, leaves of the green type are considered better tasting than those of the red.

The flower buds are edible, traditionally served steeped in soy sauce, and the seeds can be used on bread and buns, like poppy seeds.

Earth chestnut (*Bunium*) in flower

EARTH CHESTNUT (*BUNIUM BULBOCASTANUM*)

Also known as: Pig nut, Great pignut, Earth nut,
Black cumin, Black caraway.

A hardy, herbaceous perennial, the earth chestnut is a native of Europe and Asia; in the former, it was previously used as a food plant, and in the latter it still is.

ORNAMENTAL VALUE

The umbels of small, white flowers in summer are attractive – to humans and to hoverflies – and the feathery, erect, green foliage looks fresh and neat from spring to autumn. In fact, after the plant has finished flowering and setting seed in autumn, I've known it to produce new leaves from the base of the clump, and even to flower, through December and January. Earth chestnut grows about 2 feet (61 cm) high and 1 foot (30 cm) wide.

HOW TO START

Several species share this plant's common names, so be sure to buy it by its botanical Latin name. Seeds and small plants are readily available online and in some seed catalogues.

In spring, on a cool windowsill or in a cold frame outside, sow a sprinkle of seeds in seed compost in a small pot or tray. Seedlings usually appear fairly quickly; if they're not up inside three weeks, they're probably not coming. Once they're large enough to handle without difficulty, prick them out into individual small pots. It's best to leave them in their pots through their first summer, and plant them out in autumn. Some people find autumn sowing in a cold frame more effective.

You can also remove a few of the small tubers from an established clump of earth chestnut in spring or autumn, pot them up, and plant them out six months later.

Bought-in plants can be planted into their final positions on receipt in autumn or – preferably – in spring.

GROWING

Put earth chestnuts 2 feet (61 cm) apart by digging a hole, settling the plant into it so that it sits at the same depth as it was in its pot, refilling the hole around it, firming it in lightly with your fist or foot, and watering all round it. This plant also does very well in a big pot: the one I use is 12 inches (30 cm) deep and 15 inches (38 cm) across. It doesn't seem to have any real preference regarding soil type or light levels.

It's not a long-lived perennial – in my garden it lasts for about five years – so each winter collect some dry seeds from your existing plant, in order to have replacements always standing by.

The foliage grows rapidly after winter, making earth chestnut a useful, non-invasive ground cover.

PROBLEMS

I've never experienced any, or heard of any.

HARVEST & STORAGE

Leaves and shoots can be taken any time they're available. The long, curved seeds should be harvested when they're thoroughly dry, and can then be kept in a jar the same way that you store bought spices. The tubers (technically, they are tuber-like roots) are eaten in winter, while the plant is dormant. They're small and fiddly to get at, either by digging up the whole plant, assuming you've got replacements ready, or by feeling around in the soil (or, more practically, the compost of a pot) with your fingers and pulling up the small tubers. Their delicious flavour makes them well worth the effort.

EATING

The foliage tastes rather like a slightly spicy parsley and is used in a similar way, as a flavouring herb, but one that can be used in quite large quantities (provided you're not taking so much as to denude the plant).

The ripe seeds have a cumin-like flavour – or caraway, to some palates – and have been used as a substitute for that spice for centuries.

The starchy tubers, which are about 1.5 inches (4 cm) across, taste very similar to chestnuts, and are usually eaten either boiled or roasted.

Seeds forming in autumn on Red orach (*Atriplex*)

Red Orach (*Atriplex hortensis*)

Also known as: Orache, Mountain spinach, French spinach.

A fast-growing, erect, hardy annual, orach has a long history as a food crop, though nowadays it's more often seen as a bedding plant. It is thought to be one of the earliest cultivated plants, hence its species name (derived from the Latin *hortus*, meaning 'garden'), which implies that it arose through cultivation rather than in the wild.

Ornamental value

There's a grassy roundabout in our street on which the town council's gardeners often plant orach. It will be anything from 3 to 6 feet (1-2 m) tall (depending on the variety and the growing conditions) by mid-summer, and about 1 foot (30 cm) wide. The arrow-shaped leaves, about 5 inches (13 cm) long and 2-3 inches (5-7.5 cm) wide, can be found in various colours and shades, but the deep purplish reds are the types most often used, and also the ones commonly listed in seed catalogues. (There doesn't seem to be any difference in flavour between the different colours.) The flowers are tiny and dull, but the seed heads in late summer and autumn can be quite ornamental, and are attractive to finches.

How to start

Packets of seed are widely stocked, though you may need to search under orach's various names to find them. Named varieties of the redder cultivars are available. The seed is sown in small pots or trays any time from early spring to mid-summer, then pricked out into individual pots for planting out any time from late spring.

Growing

For best eating, orach needs a hearty soil, one that's rich in compost or other organic matter, plenty of moisture, and full sun. It'll survive almost anywhere, though. It looks good in a 15 inch (38 cm) patio pot, planted in peat-free multipurpose compost. It's famous for thriving in salty air, so is very useful for seaside gardens where other plants struggle.

If you want full-size plants, grow them about 18 inches (46 cm) apart, or about 8 inches (20 cm) apart for smaller specimens. Hot weather tends to prompt orach to run to seed. You can delay this inevitability to some extent by cutting off flower heads as they appear.

Problems

Orach self-seeds readily, which may or may not be a problem, depending on how neat you want or need your front garden to be. I leave the volunteer seedlings where I want them, pulling them up from where I don't want them – it's not a difficult weed to control. Self-seeding means, of course, that you only ever need to buy seed the first year.

Harvest & Storage

The younger the leaves the better they are, so start picking as soon as there's any foliage worth taking, and carry on until the flowers open, when the leaves are likely to turn tough and a little bitter. Orach doesn't store well at all, and is really only for use fresh, or frozen, blanched, as an alternative to spinach.

EATING

The soft, slightly downy leaves have the earthy taste of spinach, but milder. For this reason they're often used to bulk out a serving of a vegetable leaf such as sorrel, which may be too strong on its own, just as you might make a salad with a bit of chicory and a great pile of lettuce. Orach's main use is as a direct substitute for spinach in any recipe. As a side vegetable it's good cooked very briefly in a frying pan in butter or oil, with salt sprinkled on it during cooking. As soon as the leaves soften they're ready to serve. It also makes an excellent soup with potatoes.

Orach has a reputation for being more digestible than other 'spinaches', including spinach itself. Disappointingly, the colour doesn't survive cooking. Young, tender leaves are sometimes included in salad, more for their looks than anything.

Young foliage resprouting after first harvest of Chop suey greens (*Glebionis*)

Chop suey greens
(*Glebionis coronaria*, though often listed under its former name *Chrysanthemum coronarium*)

Also known as: Garland chrysanthemum, Shungiku, Edible chrysanthemum, Chrysanthemum greens, Crown daisy.

To anyone familiar with the foliage, flowers and smell of florists' chrysanths, this hardy annual is recognisably a chrysanthemum, though it's no longer classified as one. Of Mediterranean origin, it has sometimes been grown as an ornamental in Europe but is better known as an ingredient in Chinese and Japanese cooking. Its branching stems carry soft, strongly aromatic leaves.

Ornamental value

Leaf shape varies a little, but is commonly lobed, with a green or silvery colouring. Edible chrysanthemums have smaller flowers than the ornamental ones, about 1-2 inches (2.5-5 cm) wide. They're nothing spectacular, but they're pretty enough, usually yellow or orange, in the familiar 'sun' shape of a disc surrounded by rays. There are plenty of them, and they are visited by flying insects such as hoverflies. This plant will often carry on flowering in autumn until there's a heavy frost. In Britain it'll usually grow about a foot (30 cm) tall – double that if left to flower – with a spread of 6-10 inches (15-25 cm).

How to start

I've never seen chop suey plants for sale, but the seeds are obtainable from most seed catalogues. Sow them indoors from March, and outdoors from April, and then again in late August or September. It's not worth growing chop suey in the heart of summer, because the heat makes them bolt – that is, they produce flowers very quickly with fewer of the edible leaves, and the leaves themselves can become too bitter.

They're best started in seed trays, at a cool room temperature. Fill the tray with moist compost, sprinkle a modest pinch of seed over the surface, and cover the seeds with a thin layer of compost. They'll germinate in a couple of weeks, often much sooner in warm weather. Once the seedlings are large enough to handle confidently, transplant them to individual small pots, or to bigger trays at a spacing of a couple of inches (5 cm), and plant them out a fortnight or so later, after the frosts, when they're growing strongly.

You can also sow the seeds directly into the ground in mid-spring and early autumn, putting two or three seeds together, about 6 inches (15 cm) apart and a quarter of an inch (6 mm) deep, and later removing all but the strongest seedling at each station. In theory you can propagate this species by cuttings, as with true chrysanthemums, but I've never found it worth doing when it germinates so easily from seed. If you let them go to flower, they will sometimes self-seed.

Packets of seeds are usually sold simply as 'chop suey greens' or 'shungiku', but if you see a named cultivar being offered, do try it because it will have been bred for some improved quality.

Growing

Shungiku has a reputation for growing well in shade, but I have to say that hasn't been my experience. I've seen the plants leaning, very noticeably, towards the light, and growing weakly when I've put them in shady spots, so now I always give them a reasonably sunny position.

This is a crop that will grow in any soil but, as is so often the case, if you can place it in rich ground, or mulch it, that will help retain moisture which will make the edible parts more succulent. Chop suey greens grow well in containers – the pots don't have to be big, but the bigger they are the less often they will need watering.

Watering is important wherever you grow this vegetable because it's so quick-growing – about six weeks from sowing until eating. Because of that, its flavour, texture and yield will all suffer if it can't get enough moisture to support its rapid development.

If your chrysanthemum greens are in rows or beds, put them 6 inches (15 cm) apart, but you can plant them here and there wherever there is a gap.

The first time you harvest some leaves from a plant, make sure you take its growing tip – by which I mean the highest few inches of the stem. That'll force the plant to produce bushier growth further down its stem. You'll get a bigger and longer harvest that way, as well as more, but smaller, flowers. So, for bigger flowers, let the plants grow as they will, in which case they might need staking to stop them falling over.

This is a plant that doesn't suffer at all from moderately cold weather. It'll keep growing through the first, lesser frosts of a British autumn, and in an unheated greenhouse or under a cloche an autumn sowing is quite likely to provide greens all winter.

PROBLEMS

If you sow the seeds directly, the very youngest seedlings might be eaten by slugs and snails, although molluscs don't seem to target this species particularly. This is a noticeably trouble-free vegetable.

Chop suey greens (*Glebionis*) ready for the kitchen

HARVEST & STORAGE

I start eating my chop suey greens once they're 6 inches (15 cm) tall. The young leaves and stems are both edible. As the plant gets older the stems become tough but the leaves can still be used. You should expect to get two or three harvests from each plant, before old age begins to turn it a bit tough and bitter, though even then the tips of the foliage can still be good to eat.

My experience is that once the plants start to flower, they won't regrow no matter how you cut them back. Or rather, they might, but they'll just go straight to flower again.

EAT YOUR FRONT GARDEN

I've never found a satisfactory way of storing chop suey greens; the leaves wilt within a few hours, so pick them soon before using them.

EATING

Shungiku tastes very much like chrysanthemums smell, so before growing it as a food crop check whether you find that smell off-putting – some people do, other people love it. It's got an appetisingly bitter flavour – until the plant gets old, when it becomes just bitter, without the appetising.

The leaves and shoots are usually lightly cooked, but they can be eaten raw as a garnish or in a salad. If you find the texture in the mouth of the uncooked foliage too strange and the flavour too strong, chop suey greens can be blanched for use in salads. Plunge them into boiling water for about five seconds, then straight into very cold water long enough to get rid of the residual heat. Drain them and pat them dry.

Cooking brings out the full fragrant flavour of this unusual vegetable. Boiled, steamed or fried briefly, until just wilted, the leaves look good on the plate as they keep their shape quite well. If cooked too long they become dull, so when you're using them in something like a soup, add them just before the end of the cooking time. They're also an excellent ingredient in omelettes, stir-fries, and any dish involving rice or pasta.

The flower petals are edible, though unremarkable, and are apparently pickled in Japan, but I don't think anybody eats the disc part of the flower which is so bitter and unpleasant that you could mistake it for something you'd bought in a health shop.

Tiger nut (*Cyperus*) growing in large tubs

TIGER NUT (*CYPERUS ESCULENTUS*)

Also known as: Chufa, Yellow nutsedge, Nut grass,
Rush nut, Earth almond.

Easily mistaken for a fashionable ornamental grass, this is the source of the Spanish drink *horchata de chufa*, and was a popular tuckshop snack with British children when sweets made of sugar were rationed from 1942 to 1953. Currently, it's popular with gullible adults as a trendy 'superfood' – despite which, it is in fact tasty and nutritious.

Tiger nut is one of the oldest known cultivated plants, evidence of its use going back thousands of years. However, in many parts of the world it's best known as a terrible weed, rampant and ineradicable. It's unlikely to cause problems in the UK, but if you're gardening anywhere else you should check whether it is considered wise, or even legal, to grow it. There is a variety available (though some sources describe it as a subspecies) called *Cyperus esculentus* var. *sativus* (though some authorities seem to prefer *sativa* – look, I'm sorry, but don't blame me, blame them...). This is known to be much less prone to causing weed problems – but whether you're getting the species or the variety when you obtain either the 'nuts' (which I need hardly add are not nuts) or the plants is something you're unlikely to know unless you're buying them from a really well-organised nursery. If in doubt, I should just relocate to Britain; seriously, it's ever so nice here.

This is a herbaceous perennial, though in Britain it's usually treated as what is called a 'replant perennial', meaning that when you harvest it, you keep some of the nuts in storage, safe from frost, for replanting the following year – from the gardener's point of view it is a perennial in the sense that you only need to buy it once.

Ornamental value

I know some people who love ornamental grasses, and fill their gardens with them – and I know some people who reckon the phrase is a contradiction in terms. I think the tiger nut's clumps of fairly neat, reasonably upright, grassy leaves are attractive, and they produce a pleasant rustle on breezy days.

Chufa is sometimes grown as an ornamental in pond margins, though more commonly in tubs or open ground. From spring to autumn its numerous, long, narrow, bright green leaves reach a height of 2 or 3 feet (61 cm or 1 m), with a spread of around 8 inches (20 cm). The 'nuts', which form among the roots during the summer, are actually small tubers, ¼ to ¾ of an inch (6 to 18 mm) in length, and somewhere between round and oblong.

How to start

Until recently in this country, you had to search quite hard in gardening catalogues to find the dried tubers, which are used as if they were seed. They were more often found in health food shops, or being sold as bait for anglers. In fact, almost any source will do, if you're not bothered about which type you end up with, since the tubers, once dried, retain their viability for years.

Horchata, a drink made from ground tiger nuts

At the time of writing, however, you can not only buy the 'seeds' quite easily, you can even buy young plants, by mail order, from at least one of the main UK seed companies. I've yet to see named cultivars on sale, but I hope that would be the logical next step.

To begin from seed (we've already established that the seed nuts are neither nuts nor seeds, so I'm going to drop the inverted commas from here on to save ink), sow them singly about half an inch (12 mm) deep in pots of peat-free multipurpose compost. Do that in April under cover, or in May outdoors, for planting out in June. Otherwise, sow them directly in the garden, about 2 inches (5 cm) deep, after the last of your local spring frosts.

If you've ordered plants, they'll arrive in mid-spring. Treat them exactly as home-grown plants.

Growing

Plenty of moisture is the key to success with tiger nut. It will grow in most conditions, but you'll get bigger crops in soil or compost that is moist, or even wet. That's why, these days, I only grow them in tubs, so that I can stand their containers in trays or saucers, paddling pools or tin baths, kept topped up with water throughout the growing season. In pots or in the ground, space each plant about 10 inches (25.5 cm) from its neighbours.

They do best in a sunny position, and the nuts are said to be at their finest when grown in sandy soil, though I've never had the opportunity to test that.

As long as they're kept moist, chufa plants won't need any further attention until harvest time.

Problems

Some mice will go to a considerable effort to get at tiger nuts, whether growing or in storage. But the moat of water beneath the pot prevents access from below, while a layer of small-meshed chicken wire will prevent them getting in from above. The unsightly wire will soon be hidden from view by the growth of the plants. I've never had this difficulty myself, but if you are troubled by mice it might be an idea to use ceramic pots rather than the more chewable plastic ones.

The only other potential problem is that the stored tubers can be erratic at coming back into growth in spring. Sometimes they start so late that they haven't got enough time to form new nuts before the autumn frosts. If this happens to you, then the only foolproof answer is to buy plants instead of seeds.

EAT YOUR FRONT GARDEN

Harvest & Storage

As soon as the foliage dies back in autumn, dig up the plants, or tip them out of their pots. In a good year, you'll see hundreds of little tubers among and around the roots. They're striped, hence the common name.

Don't delay harvest too long after the leaves have gone – the tubers can rot quite quickly in frozen wet soil or compost. That's if the mice don't get them first. The other job you don't want to hang about at is washing them. It's easy enough to remove the soil from them by vigorously swishing them around in a bowl of water, provided you do it straight after lifting them. If you wait and the dirt dries and hardens, the tubers' size and shape can make cleaning them a fiddly task.

The usual way of storing the nuts – both for eating later and for next year's seed – is through dehydration, which many believe increases the flavour. You could use a dehydrator for the purpose, but I've always found they dry very easily without any added heat. I spread them out in a layer at cool room temperature, and within a week or so they are as hard as gravel.

You can also store them for a winter without drying them, by burying them in moist sand, in a cool but frost-free shed or garage. For use as next year's seed, they do need to be dried.

Eating

Tiger nuts are eaten raw, cooked, dried, ground or liquidised. There are lots of recipes online for the sweet, refreshing, non-alcoholic drink called *horchata*, which is made of tiger nuts, water and flavouring. An extremely simple and tasty alternative to dairy or soya milk is made by liquidising 8 ounces (227 g) of tiger nuts with

Tiger nut (*Cyperus*) tubers harvested, washed, and ready for drying

2 pints (1.14 litres) of cold water. Leave the mixture to stand for 5 or 6 hours, and then strain off the liquid, which is now ready for use.

If you're eating your tiger nuts raw, be warned – they are hard on the teeth. Even cooked they don't soften all that much. I imagine that's why some people prefer to soak them in water and then mash them. They are often cooked by boiling, for use as an ingredient or a snack, or roasted as if they really were nuts.

They have an excellent, strong but never overpowering flavour – I don't know anyone who doesn't like them – which is definitely nutty, and in which people variously detect vanilla, almond and coconut. They're also sweet, without being sickly, and because they are so rich in oil they make a satisfying food. But if you've got fragile teeth, you might be best advised to suck rather than chew.

Rock samphire (*Crithmum*) growing in a 12 inch pot

Rock samphire (*Crithmum maritimum*)

Also known as: Sea fennel, True samphire.

A hardy perennial in the wild, though sometimes treated as a hardy annual or half-hardy perennial in gardens, rock samphire is a plant of sandy beaches, rocks and shingle, and cliffs. Eaten since time immemorial by coastal dwellers, for centuries it was a free food for the poor, and a dangerous cash crop for the brave: precariously gathered from cliffs by pickers lowered on ropes, samphire was brined in barrels for the London trade. Today, so I'm told, it can be spotted punctuating the white open expanses of expensively empty plates in fancy restaurants.

It still grows in various parts of the British coastline, though not as commonly as it once did. It's sometimes suggested that the only reason people stopped eating it in the late nineteenth century was because it was over-harvested until there wasn't enough left growing wild to be worth picking. These days, it is illegal to gather wild rock samphire in the UK. It's sometimes found growing, self-sown, in the sunny walls of seaside gardens, or deliberately planted in rock gardens.

Ornamental value

As a garden plant, rock samphire will grow to between 6 inches (15 cm) and 2 feet (61 cm) tall, in spreading, aromatic patches made up of solid, smooth, branching stems and fleshy, divided leaves. Both stems and leaves are of a vibrant green, or sometimes a grey-green or blue-green. Beautiful and strange, they form frondy antlers, kept upright and firm by their succulence. It's a foliage plant for people who enjoy shape as well as colour.

In summer it produces umbels of small, green-yellow flowers, reminiscent of the flowers of dill or fennel.

Samphire does tend to look a bit tatty during the winter, I'm afraid, though in mild winters in mild gardens it will sometimes remain green throughout the year.

How to start

So as not to confuse *Crithmum* with various unrelated species also known commonly as samphire, make sure you buy it by its botanical name. Seeds are listed in some vegetable and herb catalogues, and some wildflower catalogues. I have only rarely seen young plants for sale online.

Use peat-free seed compost for sowing – not multipurpose, because it holds too much water. To aid drainage I usually mix in some horticultural sand (see Resources, pages 234-5), using one part sand to two parts compost. Fill a 4 inch (10 cm) pot, put it in a pot saucer and fill the saucer with water. Place seeds on the surface of the compost, pressing them in lightly so that they are in full contact with the compost, and leaving half an inch (12 mm) or so between each seed. Cover them with a light sprinkling of compost, so that they're invisible but not deeply buried. Sowing can take place in spring or autumn.

The compost needs to be moist, but never actually wet, for as long as the seeds or seedlings are in it. I realise that's one of those annoyingly imprecise instructions often found in gardening books. Perhaps the easiest way to know whether you've got it right is to pick up the pot daily and check underneath it: there should never be any

Rock samphire (*Crithmum*) seedlings ready for pricking out

water sitting in the saucer, or visible on the bottom of the pot, but at the same time the surface of the compost should never be dry. Leave the pot in the saucer, and use that whenever more moisture is needed – never water the pot from above.

Keep the pot somewhere that is light and frost-free, but not warm, such as a cold frame or an unheated greenhouse or unheated conservatory, or – failing all the above – a windowsill in a cool room.

Germination can be slow – I've known it take ten weeks from an April sowing, though three or four is more usual. When the seedlings are large enough to handle without risk of squashing, transplant them into individual 3 inch (7.5 cm) pots. This time use a peat-free multipurpose compost, though again, mixing in some sand (about one part in four) may help drainage. Continue to keep the pots somewhere frost-free and light.

I know some gardeners who've had success by sowing the large seeds directly where they are to grow, especially by poking them into gaps in a south-facing, drystone wall. Rock samphire will self-sow if growing in particularly favourable conditions.

GROWING

There isn't much literature on how to grow rock samphire, so I've mostly had to learn it over the years from trial and error. In other words, my way of doing it might not be the best way. But if my advice doesn't work for you, do feel free to experiment.

I always let my samphires stay undercover throughout their first winter, potting them on to slightly larger pots if they get too big for the ones they're in, so they can get really well established, showing plenty of foliage. Whether I've sown them in spring or autumn, I won't plant them out until the following spring or summer.

Although it's a seaside plant in the wild, in cultivation rock samphire can grow anywhere provided it has good drainage. It also needs to be in full sun, or as close to full as you can manage – meaning, a position which gets as many hours per day of sunlight as possible, as opposed to shade. Space the plants about a foot (30 cm) apart.

Above all, with rock samphire you should always be looking for a spot of ground that has good drainage. If its roots get saturated, it dies. By 'good drainage', I mean that whatever water falls on the soil (from watering or from rain) goes through it rapidly, instead of sitting visibly on the surface. Ten minutes after the rain has stopped, there should be no puddles on the ground; an hour later, if you stick your finger a couple of inches into the soil, it shouldn't emerge with mud clinging to it.

The ground chosen for rock samphire needs to dry out periodically; this is not a plant that's going to be troubled by drought. Rich, moisture-retentive, organic soil – the sort you seek out for almost all vegetables – won't do here. (To confuse things further, what you would ideally use is soil that is both rich *and* light, and if you've got that, is it OK if I move in with you?)

If you haven't got a suitable patch of soil, you can make a pocket to plant into by digging a bowl-shaped hole with a spade, and before you refill it, mixing in with the displaced soil an equal volume of coarse horticultural grit (which is sold at garden centres and DIY stores).

Those who possess a sunny garden wall with crevices into which they can plant their samphire don't need to worry about drainage – the wall will take care of all that on its own. If you've got a slope in your garden, planting samphire at the top of it should also aid drainage, by allowing excess water to run off.

For the rest of us, using a pot that's about 12-15 inches (30-38 cm) in diameter and at least a foot (30 cm) deep can be the best solution. Fill the container with the same mixture of sand and peat-free multipurpose compost mentioned earlier.

It's often claimed that samphire needs to be watered with salt water, but this seems very unlikely to me. Coastal species like this one are tolerant of salty water, but that doesn't mean they need it or even benefit from it. I use the rain-butt, and when that's empty I switch to tap water.

Cut flowering stems right back to the base of the plant as soon as they have finished blooming.

PROBLEMS

Legion, to be frank – although I am glad to tell you that at least I have never encountered any pests or diseases on rock samphire.

The seeds often have a poor rate of germination, even when fresh, and old seed is more or less hopeless. Buy new seed every year, or better yet save seed from your own plants and sow it as soon as it's ripe.

The seedlings often don't survive transplanting, which is why I let them grow on until they're quite sturdy before planting them out.

I have lost samphire plants during a severe winter, but I don't think it's the cold that kills, so much as that the frozen ground doesn't dry out well enough. Even so, any inland garden is likely to be frostier than samphire's natural coastal habitat, so covering plants with a cloche in cold winters might be worth a try. If you're using pots, you might try moving them to shelter during the worst weather, such as a cold frame or greenhouse, or just in the lee of a house wall.

Harvest & Storage

Cut sprigs with scissors from mid-spring to mid-autumn when the plant is growing strongly. Late spring and early summer will usually be the times of heaviest picking. Take the young growth, which is lighter in colour, as older leaves can become a bit tough. Samphire will keep in the fridge for a day or two, but not much longer in crisp condition.

It'll freeze reasonably well, but the best way to store rock samphire – and historically the most popular way of eating it – is pickled. There is, perhaps, no better pickle than rock samphire; it retains a firm texture, and most importantly it is one of the very few things I've ever pickled in which the dominant flavour of the finished product is of the vegetable rather than of the vinegar. There are lots of pickling recipes online, but here's the one I use for one of the simplest, quickest, tastiest and best-looking pickles you'll ever make.

Pickled rock samphire – perfect with Stilton

Sterilise a small pickling jar or jam jar by washing it in hot, soapy water, rinsing thoroughly in hot water, and then drying it in an oven at 275 °F / 140 °C / Gas Mark 1 for ten minutes. (The size of the jar, of course, depends on the amount of samphire available to pick that day, so prepare two or three jars in case one alone isn't big enough. I find a large handful of samphire fills one 250 ml jar.)

Pick your samphire, wash it in cold water and pat it dry with a tea towel. In a large saucepan put 300 ml of cider vinegar, a bay leaf and a teaspoon of black peppercorns. Bring the vinegar to the boil and simmer it for five minutes. Take the pan off the stove, and stir the samphire into the vinegar. Immediately pack the samphire and peppercorns into the jar, pour in as much of the hot vinegar as needed to fill it up, and seal the jar. Leave for at least a month before eating. It'll keep in a cool, dark cupboard for six months. Once a jar is opened, keep it in the fridge and use it up in about a month. Stilton, water biscuits and pickled rock samphire: most leading philosophers agree that this is the true meaning of Christmas.

EATING

Rock samphire is a very strong-flavoured vegetable, so if you don't like it you'll probably not like it quite a lot. However, as with many peculiar, unfamiliar tastes, it seems to grow on people who may have recoiled on first whiff.

Flavours that people mention when trying to describe samphire include salt, asparagus, carrot, lemon – and kerosene. I think kerosene is a bit unfair, but it's true to say that if you've ever smelled the polish they use on the wooden pews of rural Anglican churches, this vegetable's resinous smell and taste (greatly prized by our ancestors, remember) may remind you of it.

To get the full experience the first time you grow it, steam it and then eat it unadorned, tossed in melted butter. As an ingredient, rather than used on its own, rock samphire gives a lovely smell and taste, not overpowering as you might expect, and has a pleasing, firm texture. Try it in stir-fries, omelettes, scrambled eggs, or any cheese dish, or use it chopped, like chives, into butter to dress a potato in its jacket.

Usually cooked, briefly, before use, by boiling, steaming or blanching, rock samphire can also be used as a garnish, like parsley, or sparingly in salads. Visually, it is a real appetiser, maintaining its shape and intense colour even when cooked or pickled.

Chinese water celery (*Oenanthe*) in a large plastic tub

CHINESE WATER CELERY
(*OENANTHE JAVANICA* 'FLAMINGO')

Also known as: Water celery, Japanese parsley,
Variegated water dropwort.

A hardy perennial bog plant, water celery is a widely-grown aquatic ornamental in the UK, and a common vegetable in many parts of the East, especially Japan and Korea. Its hollow, creeping stems, with roots at every node, rapidly form a dense, floating raft covered with foliage, spreading across the surface of the water in its container. It is often used as a marginal plant in ponds. Water celery also grows vigorously in permanently wet soil, so can be used for ground cover.

ORNAMENTAL VALUE

The feathery, variegated foliage is present from early spring to early winter, or sometimes all year round in mild conditions. The small, finely cut individual leaves are light green with rosy pink and creamy white margins. The colours change somewhat through the seasons, with stronger shades appearing in the cooler night-time temperatures of spring and autumn. Water celery is especially spectacular in autumn, when the whole clump is covered with foliage, flowers and seed heads. It is 12-16 inches (30-40 cm) tall when in flower. The umbels of small, white flowers, rather like cow parsley, appear in summer.

How to start

Several species in this genus are very poisonous, so make sure you buy Flamingo by its botanical name, from a reputable, established supplier. Young plants are widely available online and from nurseries in early spring and through the summer. They can be planted out at any time except winter.

Propagation by taking divisions from existing plants is so easy as to be almost an insult to the skilled gardener. One autumn, as an experiment, I tore some bits of floating stems at random out of an established pot, and dumped them – literally dropped them – into a shallow plastic container in which I'd put a couple of inches of garden mud topped up with tap water. They were growing away within a week. Autumn seems the obvious time for dividing, but I imagine it could also be done in spring.

Growing

I'd love to fill a couple of pages with all the complicated ministrations needed to keep this plant going, but to be honest there just isn't anything more to say – stick it in a tub of water, walk away, and that's about it. Later on, you eat it. Perhaps you could…no, sorry, can't think of anything. I suppose in a drought you might need to top the water up, but really that's hardly worth mentioning so I won't bother. Only now does it begin to dawn on me that I should have saved this easy species for a future book called *Gardening for People Who Don't Want to do any Gardening*.

I started mine one summer by taking a round, plastic tub, 15 inches (40 cm) deep by 21 inches (53 cm) across – one with no drainage holes in it – and half filling it with soil from an unused patch of the garden. (If you haven't got any soil, buy a bag of aquatic

Garden flexi-trug half filled with mud for planting Chinese water celery into

compost from a garden centre.) I added enough water to make the soil muddy, knocked the water celery out of the small pot it had arrived in, and planted it into the mud, at roughly the same level as it had been in the pot. Finally, I added more water to the tub so that the soil level was submerged by about 4 inches (10 cm).

Within a month, the water celery had spread to cover about half the surface of the pot, and its tallest leaves were 3 inches (7.5 cm) above the water. It was already an attractive planting, with those cheerful colours that gardeners of a certain generation last saw in a 1970s sweetshop.

If you're growing it in the ground, allow each plant 2 feet (61 cm) of space – a gap it should fill in its first year – and make sure the soil never dries out.

Water celery must have a sunny position, and the more sun you can offer it, the stronger the growth and the brighter the colours. You can trim the foliage whenever you wish to keep the plant in the desired shape and condition, or just rely on regular harvesting of the leaves to do the job.

Problems

As far as growing is concerned, this plant is completely trouble-free and more or less effort-free. It can be invasive, but since I grow it on its own in a tub standing on the drive, that's not something I have to worry about. If the mass of rooty stems curling round and round the inside of the top of the pot looks as if it's becoming too much, I use secateurs to cut out handfuls of it for the compost bin.

Harvest & Storage

Whenever the foliage is present, you can harvest it as required, cutting sprigs of leaf and stalk as you would with parsley. It'll certainly be available to take through most of spring and autumn, and all of summer. It may be available during winter, though I've known heavy frosts to kill off all the foliage that's standing proud of the water.

Water celery doesn't store well at all.

Eating

The aromatic leaves are used both raw and cooked. As with so many crops, the younger leaves are good in salads, and the older ones are better as cooked greens, boiled or steamed for around a minute. Water celery makes a good seasoning for soups and rice dishes.

The flavour reminds different people of carrot, celery or parsley, with a slightly spicy tang to it. The cooked foliage is milder than the raw. Really young water celery leaves, just picked, in a peanut butter sandwich – that's the sort of food they'd serve at state banquets if they only knew of it.

Chinese yam (*Dioscorea*)

SECTION THREE

PLANTS GROWN MAINLY AS CLIMBERS

Mashua (*Tropaeolum tuberosum*) climbing a wire mesh fence

Mashua (*Tropaeolum tuberosum*)

Also known as: Tuberous nasturtium, Machua, Anu.

One of the four great root crops of the Andean region – along with potatoes, oca (see pages 197-203), and ulluco – this close relative of the nasturtium has been cultivated for its highly nutritious tubers for thousands of years. Outside its native region it's more often grown as an ornamental, although every few years someone tries to introduce it to Europe as a horticultural crop. It never quite catches on.

When I first grew mashua in the early 1990s it was undergoing one of its occasional revivals in popularity amongst British gardeners. But since then it has been overshadowed (at least in the small world of Andean tubers that are grown on British allotments) by oca, and I can understand why. Oca does tend to be more reliable in our climate than either mashua or ulluco – it often gives bigger yields, and most people find it easier to store over the winter for replanting in spring. Added to which, oca is generally listed in catalogues as a vegetable, whereas mashua generally isn't. For many of us, however, mashua is such an unusual and enjoyable vegetable that it's worth a bit of bother.

Ornamental value

Mashua is a tender perennial which disappears over winter. In the UK it's usually grown as a 'replant perennial', the tubers being lifted for storage after the first autumn frosts and replanted after the last spring frosts.

It's a scrambling climber, which will easily make 6 feet (2 m) in height, and spread for about a yard (1 m) in several directions. It's at its best on a fence. In fact, buy the ugliest fence you can afford, because then you'll get even more pleasure from seeing it hidden by the mashua. The leaves are similar to nasturtium leaves, but with a slightly tidier, more 'formal' appearance.

In summer, mashua produces numerous trumpet-shaped, bicoloured flowers, orange with reddish backs, which last until the plant is cut down by frost.

HOW TO START

Mashua is grown from tubers, rarely from seed, and you'll usually find it in catalogues of ornamental climbers, probably listed under its botanical name. That makes it a perfect subject for this book, which is concerned with crypto-vegetables – edibles that hide in plain sight pretending to be ornamentals.

Make sure you get a cultivar named 'Ken Aslet', as this one has been bred to succeed in British conditions. Most other mashuas are day-length sensitive, which means they only start flowering and forming their tubers (the part we use for food and propagation) in the autumn, which in temperate climates doesn't give them enough time to finish the job before winter starts. (Ken Aslet, incidentally, was a famous plant collector who worked at the Royal Horticultural Society in the middle of the last century.)

Try not to order your tubers until mid-spring; let the company you buy them from take on the burden of keeping them alive over winter rather than struggling with it yourself.

Mashua can be planted directly in the soil, but I always prefer to start them in pots, to protect them against slugs and snails which can be a problem during the earliest stages of growth. I put each tuber in a 4 inch (10 cm) pot of peat-free multipurpose compost in March, April or May – towards the end of that period if I think the tubers still look healthy, and earlier if I fear that they are beginning to soften or wrinkle. The tuber should be covered by not more than about an inch (2.5 cm) of compost. Orientation of the tuber – whether you plant it upright or horizontally – doesn't appear to make any difference. Keep the pots somewhere light and frost-free, but reasonably cool – in an unheated spare room, for instance, or in a greenhouse or conservatory.

At this stage – and to be frank, this is one reason why some gardeners prefer to *avoid* this stage – the main danger is from overwatering, which will quickly rot the tuber. It's a slightly difficult balance to get right, but keeping the compost too dry will always be better than keeping it too wet. When I overwater potted tubers it's almost invariably due to impatience – mashua shoots can take several weeks to appear, and sometimes the temptation to add a little water, just to try and get the process started, is too much for me.

Even after the shoots appear, potted mashuas can still rot from overwatering, so don't water at all unless you're sure the compost is dry. The underneath of the pot can be more telling than the surface of the compost; if there's any moisture at all around the drainage holes, or on the pot saucer where the pot's been standing, then the compost is wet enough. Or possibly too wet…

I have sometimes found mashua tubers both rotting *and* shooting (or rooting) simultaneously. What I do then is carefully repot the tuber in dry compost, and the resulting race between rotting and growing is, as often as not, won by the forces of progress.

GROWING

With most plants, you look at the bottom of the pot to see if roots

Mashua (*Tropaeolum tuberosum*) in full bloom

are showing through the drainage holes – that's when you know the plant is ready for potting on or planting out. But I find mashua will grow several inches tall and still show nothing underneath, so I just go by the foliage, the date and the weather. If, in mid- or late spring, when the soil has warmed up and you aren't expecting any more frosts, the top of the plant looks vibrant and well-established, then it's ready to go.

If you're planting the tubers direct, rather than via small pots, again wait until you can be pretty sure there are no more frosts coming, and the soil isn't cold to the touch. Where I garden, in Somerset, that's usually during the second half of May or early June. Put them about 1 foot (30 cm) apart, and just an inch or two (2.5-5 cm) below the soil.

If you're planting your mashua from a pot into the ground, then

EAT YOUR FRONT GARDEN

dig a hole slightly bigger than the pot with a trowel or hand-fork. Tip the plant out of the pot, complete with its compost, and put it in the hole. It should be planted at roughly the same depth in the ground as it was in the pot. Refill the hole with soil, and water the plant in thoroughly to settle it into the ground.

As long as the soil is free-draining, and never gets soggy or boggy, but also doesn't dry out completely in summer, any ground will grow mashua. For best results, though, try to find a patch that's rich and deep. Forking in a few bucketfuls of thoroughly-rotted manure or garden compost will help a lot.

The plants will grow in sun or in light shade, but ideally you want the foliage to be in the sunshine, while the roots are in the shade. That's why people often grow mashua amongst low shrubs or ground-cover plants, so that it's permanently shady around the roots but the tops can climb up to find the sun. My experience has always been that the top growth isn't much affected by shade or sun, but that the size and number of tubers is significantly greater in a sunny spot.

Mashua grows pretty well in patio pots (the bigger the tub the better, with a minimum volume of about 30 litres), but I always get bigger plants, and bigger crops of bigger tubers, from plants that are grown in the ground. This is probably because, no matter how diligently you water a container, ground-grown crops will almost always be able to get their moisture more easily and consistently. When you harvest a pot of mashua you'll see that the plant only seems to use the top few inches of compost – that's where the tubers and roots are found. However, I've noticed that they don't thrive in shallow containers, presumably because without a reasonable depth, the compost dries out too often.

Once they're safely planted out, mashuas will grow at an impressive rate of several inches a week even in relatively poor weather, especially if you can place them somewhere where they have some shelter from the wind. They climb very readily by wrapping their stems around anything they touch, such as a wire fence, a trellis, rough sticks (but not smooth poles), or – and this is perhaps how they look their best – when left to find their own way up and through neighbouring bushes and small trees. But do watch out that the plant doesn't grasp and pull down the stems of flowers and other delicate neighbours.

If you don't want your mashua to climb, you can just leave it to sprawl over the ground, but by growing it vertically you'll keep the foliage out of the reach of slugs and snails, save space in the garden, and display its leaves and flowers to best effect.

There isn't much else that needs doing between planting and harvesting. Mashua foliage is usually quite dense at the bottom of the plant, so weeds are rarely a problem. Earthing-up around the plants as they grow – the way you do with potatoes – is not necessary, but many growers claim it increases yields. Plentiful watering during dry spells is helpful, as is mulching around the base of the plant with garden compost once it's growing strongly.

Sometimes, in a very hot, dry summer – even a British summer – mashua goes dormant. Don't worry: keep watering, and when the weather cools a bit the plants will come back to life.

All the above makes mashua sound like a tricky thing to grow, but there are many years when I just plant it without much fuss, and it grows like mad without any problems. In theory these ought to be the years when conditions suit it best, but as any gardener knows plants grow less predictably than that. There must be smaller variations than the ones we're able to note, which have a great effect. For instance, where I live, 2017 was a summer of two periods of unseasonal heatwaves, weeks of very heavy rain, and two quite serious gales – but all my mashua plants produced astonishing crops, covering the fences with perfect, undamaged foliage, and with flowers in layered cascades as if organised by a master topiarist who'd retrained as a high society flower arranger (but not because of a scandal or anything, he just fancied a change). That year, my mashua grew – without any setback on its part, or any effort on my part – as a climber and as ground cover in open spaces, pest-free and rampant.

PROBLEMS

There are two creatures which I have had a lot of trouble with on mashua. First, the caterpillars of Large White butterflies (one of two species which are often referred to collectively as 'Cabbage Whites') can strip a growing mashua plant in mid-summer to a leafless skeleton. When that happens, I give the plant a feed with a proprietary seaweed solution and, once the caterpillars have moved on, more often than not it will recover, the foliage will regrow, and by early autumn the only sign of what happened is that the individual leaves tend to be smaller than they were before the caterpillars arrived.

Blackfly also attacks in mid-summer, and a really heavy infestation of this aphid can make a plant collapse in just a few days. I have known mashua recover from blackfly, but not so often. This seems to be much more of a problem in containers than in the open ground.

There are plenty of books and websites which will give you suggestions for dealing with such pests, and you must follow whichever seems most acceptable to you. (Personally, I apply the 'Kitten Test' to pest control: if you wouldn't be willing to do it to a kitten, you shouldn't be willing to do it to a slug, an aphid or a caterpillar, otherwise you are guilty of sentimentality, inconsistency, and perhaps even hypocrisy. But that's just me – we all draw our own lines in our own sand.)

On the allotment, vegetables can be completely protected from caterpillars with netting or fleece (if it's well enough applied and maintained), but that isn't really practical with a climbing plant like mashua, and in any case it would rather defeat the purpose of this book by making your front garden look like a vegetable patch.

HARVEST & STORAGE

The usual advice is to wait until autumn frosts kill the foliage, then to cut all the dead stuff off with secateurs before carefully lifting the tubers with a garden fork. And that advice is correct, as far as it goes – but for many of us these days there is a complication. Certainly where I live, our typical autumn weather is now so warm that November, and even December, can be spent in a frustrating, fruitless wait for a frost hard enough to freeze a mashua's top growth.

Sometimes, around Christmas, I just decide to dig the plants up anyway. This can't be ideal – if the plants haven't been frosted they're less likely to enter dormancy for the winter, and so will be harder to store. But if you wait too long, there's a danger that the tubers will rot in wet soil, or be attacked by slugs. (Of course, this only applies to the tubers you're planning to store: those for immediate eating can be taken any time in autumn, with or without frosts, as soon as they're of a useable size.)

If you do garden in an area where warm autumns are becoming a problem, I think the only answer is to put your eggs in as many baskets as possible. Lift some of the tubers in November or December, whether or not there's been a hard frost; lift more once the frost finally arrives; and leave some of them in the ground (or pot) throughout the winter, mulched with 3 or 4 inches (7-10 cm) of compost, leaves, bracken, straw or shredded paper. Although tender, in many areas mashua will survive in the ground over winter this

EAT YOUR FRONT GARDEN

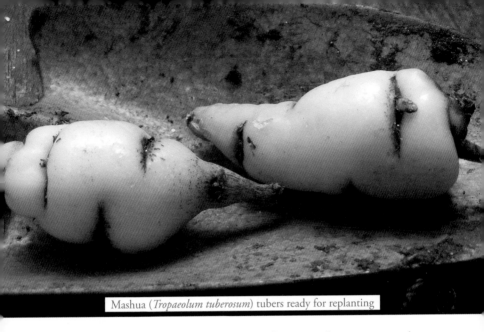

Mashua (*Tropaeolum tuberosum*) tubers ready for replanting

way. At least, it'll survive the freezing – but it might not survive the damp and the slugs.

It's usually not difficult to lift a few of the tubers, leaving the rest undisturbed, because most of them grow quite near the surface, and if the soil (or compost in a pot) is loose enough you'll be able to feel around with your fingers and snap off individual tubers. If you are digging them up with a fork, though, make sure you put it in a boot-length or so from the base of the plant, to avoid spearing the tubers on its tines.

What you'll find as you turn the soil over will delight your eyes. Mashua tubers are oblong, and quite small – about 5 inches (12-13 cm) is a very respectable length, though you'll see them larger and smaller than that. The underlying colour of their waxy skins is a kind of ivory white, but they are often, and variously, mottled, flushed, striped and spotted with reds and greens. The flesh inside is yellowish.

Yields are very variable, but can be impressive in a good year. A couple of pounds (a kilogram) per plant is a reasonable ambition, though sometimes it'll be much more or much less.

After one warm, wet summer in the mid-1990s I had such a huge crop of tubers – thirty of good size, plus a few tiddlers, from one plant alone – that I was able to supply some back to the nurseryman I'd bought the original stock from. He'd lost all his to a late frost. As you can imagine, I felt very proud of myself. The following spring, by way of thanks, he sent me a big bag of his tubers – which was handy, because that year I'd lost every one of mine. They'd all rotted over the winter.

If the harvested tubers are at all damp from being in the soil, let them dry for a few days, open to the air at room temperature. After that, storing tubers for eating in the near future is fairly simple. They'll keep in a plastic bag in the fridge for a week or two – and for several weeks if you use Green Bags (see Resources, pages 234-5).

Storing mashua for longer – whether for next year's 'seed', or to eat later in the winter – is harder. It must be admitted, they're not always the easiest tubers to keep alive and healthy over the winter. Again, I'd recommend trying several methods and locations to see which one works best for you. In a ventilated pantry or larder, on a shelf in a dry, frost-free garage, or in a cool spare room, put some tubers in a paper bag, or a hessian sack. Others can be buried in slightly moist compost or sand in plant pots, or in cardboard boxes. (That's clean, bought-in compost, fresh from the bag; and horticultural sand – see Resources, pages 234-5.)

Only store tubers that are in perfect condition, without any wounds – and choose larger ones if possible. Whether or not large 'seed' tubers produce large crops is debatable, but they certainly keep better than smaller ones, perhaps because it takes them longer to dry out.

With luck – and luck really does seem to figure in this – your tubers should keep for six months.

EAT YOUR FRONT GARDEN

EATING

The leaves and flowers of mashua are, like those of nasturtium, edible, and some people do eat them. I find them greatly inferior to nasturtium, and prefer to leave them in place doing their respective jobs of feeding the plant and brightening the garden.

The tubers are another matter: strange and lovely, quite different to any other food I've ever tasted. When you bite into a raw, fresh mashua (fresh tubers aren't usually peeled, while stored tubers usually are) it's crunchy and juicy like a radish, and there's a fragrant taste of vanilla and aniseed. There's a slight, mustard-like heat, but more peppery than that, as if from watercress – or, obviously, nasturtium. The overall taste, though, can't be fully described by comparing it with others. It is unique. Oh, and I probably ought to mention that quite a lot of people *really* hate it.

You can also do what the Andeans do: leave the tubers somewhere sunny for a fortnight, which will reduce the mustard flavour and increase the sweetness. They are also frozen to sweeten them – in Bolivia, mashua is traditionally served frozen and covered with molasses. Must be honest: I haven't tried that one.

In any case, the tubers become quite different when cooked, a bit reminiscent of Jerusalem artichoke, chestnut, and carrot. They can be boiled, parboiled and then fried, roasted, steamed, baked, used in stews, casseroles and soups, or served as if they were new potatoes. They don't need much cooking – a 10 minute boil or steam is plenty.

It's said that in the Andes, well-to-do urban people shun mashua because they consider it a peasant food, associated with poor 'natives'. Isn't it strange how peasant food is always so much tastier than the muck that posh people eat?

Apios is a vigorous climber in spring and summer

Apios (*Apios americana*)

Also known as: Indian potato, Hodoimo, Potato bean, Groundnut
(though this name is also used for several other species).

Centuries ago, this hardy, herbaceous perennial was a major food in North America ('Indian' potato refers to the native peoples of America, not of India), and is reputed to be one of the wild plants that saved early European colonists from winter starvation after they were introduced to it by kindly locals. It appears above ground between the last frosts of spring and the first frosts of autumn as a vine, which climbs by twining.

Ornamental value

From late summer into autumn, scented flowers of pink, purple or reddish-brown bloom in dense clusters, 3-5 inches (7.5-13 cm) long. Apios is a member of the pea and bean family, as you can tell from the flowers which look rather like those of runner beans.

The foliage is pinnate, meaning that the leaflets are arranged either side of the stalk. Each leaf is from 3-6 inches (7.5-15 cm) long, becoming larger and more numerous as the plant gets older. They open and fold according to the amount of sun available, and droop in heavy rain. The vines can easily reach 8 feet (2.5 m) tall when established.

How to start

Apios can be grown from seed, though I've never seen it for sale in this country. Tubers and young plants are sold by several online nurseries – they can be planted at any time other than winter, but I recommend ordering them in late winter (before stocks run out) for planting in late spring.

Once a plant is two or three years old it will produce numerous tubers every year. Every one of these tubers, of any size, is capable of producing a new plant, so this is a crop you should only ever need to buy once. For propagation purposes, harvest tubers in early spring, and put them singly in small pots of peat-free multipurpose compost, planted 3 or 4 inches (7.5-10 cm) deep. Keep them under cover, such as in an unheated greenhouse or a cold frame, until May.

Spring works best for propagation, but you can also pot up the tubers in autumn and leave them outside for the winter. They'll appear the following spring.

GROWING

Plant apios outside in May, 12 inches (30 cm) apart, with tubers 4 inches (10 cm) deep, and young plants at the same depth as they were in their pots.

Harvesting the tubers is a lot easier if you grow apios in a container filled with peat-free multipurpose compost. It'll grow in any size of pot, but the bigger the tub the bigger the crop. I've had good results from one that's 15 inches (38 cm) deep and the same across.

If you prefer to grow it in the ground, choose moist, rich soil if possible, though apios will do all right in any soil that isn't very dry (you can still grow it in a dry position, of course, by keeping it in a tub). It'll grow particularly well in heavy and even boggy soil, where most vegetables would struggle – though in that case, good luck with harvesting the tubers.

The scented flowers of Apios

Wherever you plant it, it must have plenty of sunlight. Having said that, this is a plant that chases the light, so it will climb up, through and along anything it can get hold of, to put its leaves in the sunniest position it can find. To keep it neat, plant it in a sunny position with a fence to twine onto. In the absence of a fence, you can use sticks, beanpoles, trellis or ornamental 'climbing frames'. If you don't want it climbing randomly through neighbouring plants, keep an eye on it and regularly tie it into its own supports.

Never allow the soil or compost to dry out. It takes a lot of water to produce big groundnuts, so water once a week in hot weather – the plant will lose its leaves in summer if it's too dry. Otherwise, apios is cultivated with little effort. Once the vines appear in April, May or June they will grow quickly, and weeds are unlikely to be troublesome except in the first couple of years when the plants are still quite small. Like other legumes, it provides its own nitrogen and doesn't need feeding.

PROBLEMS

None.

HARVEST & STORAGE

Harvest tubers for eating in autumn or winter, after frost has withered the vines. The groundnuts form as lumps along the length of stringy roots, like a necklace or a string of sausages, growing out from the plant. Conveniently, most of them are found no deeper than 6 inches (15 cm), with some in the top couple of inches. They tend to be somewhere between round and oval, shaped a bit like Obelix's menhirs.

The tubers vary in diameter and length; I've had them from the size of a shelled peanut to that of a small potato. They're probably best taken for eating at around the size of a walnut or golf ball; the very biggest can have a disappointing, slightly spongy texture. Unharvested, the little tubers get bigger each year, and it's a good idea to leave a new plant alone for the first year or two until some of the tubers are big enough to be worth bothering with. All the tubers

Edible tubers of Apios

can be eaten – the big one that you originally planted, or the smaller ones that the plant has since produced to spread itself. Whether it's new ones from this year or those that have been growing for a few seasons, it's size alone that matters.

If your apios is growing in the ground, harvest by feeling around in the soil with your fingers and gently pulling out the bumpy strings. Any tubers left behind deliberately or accidentally will gradually increase the spread of your apios patch.

This method works for pot-grown plants as well, but with them there's also an easier way: tip the whole contents of the container into a larger trug, a wheelbarrow, or even a cardboard box, and then just sift through by hand, removing those tubers you want to eat. Dump the compost back into the container, along with the tubers that you haven't harvested. You could replant them as before for best results, but it's not that important to do so – they'll find their own level.

The groundnuts will keep in a plastic bag in the fridge for at least a fortnight, but if you leave them in the ground or the pot they'll keep perfectly right through until spring.

Eating

The smooth-skinned tubers are very easily cleaned by lightly scrubbing in water, revealing an attractive skin that reminds me of a hardwood that's been treated with wood stain. They don't need peeling. Cut one in half, and you'll see, beneath the skin, firm, white flesh.

Apios is eaten cooked, usually boiled, baked or roasted. I like them steamed, whole, for ten minutes. As the common name 'Indian potato' suggests, they can then be employed in most of the same ways that spuds are, though the flesh is of a thick, soft texture, more fibrous than potatoes, with a pleasant, smooth feel on the tongue. The skin remains crisp.

As you cut into a tuber it has an inviting smell of baked potato, sweet potato, and chestnut. It tastes of chestnut and sweet potato, too, a mild but really delicious, slightly nutty flavour.

Apios is good in soups and stews, or as a potato-like vegetable on its own. It mashes superbly. A traditional use was to dry the tubers and grind them to flour, for baking or as thickener for soups and sauces. The plant is known as the 'Potato bean' because the seeds are also eaten in America; plants may occasionally produce small crops of seedpods in Britain, but mine never have.

Chinese yam (*Dioscorea*)

Chinese yam (*Dioscorea batatas*)

Also known as: Cinnamon vine, Dioscorea opposita,
D. polystachya.

Most members of this genus of twining climbers are tropical or subtropical plants, and though they are important food crops throughout much of the world, they are unsuitable for growth in temperate regions. This particular species, however, is easy to grow as a hardy herbaceous perennial in Britain, where it is sometimes seen as an ornamental, and occasionally as a vegetable.

Ornamental value

This is a very attractive vine, which can easily reach 6 feet (2 m) tall and a foot (30 cm) wide in a season. It has glossy leaves up to 4 inches (10 cm) long, in an elongated heart shape, and smooth green or reddish stems. It is perfect for covering a chain-link fence, or screening an eyesore through the summer months.

Its above-ground growth disappears during winter and reappears towards the end of spring, after which growth is rapid. It's at its most ornamental in autumn, with a sort of upside-down fountain of pinkish and golden foliage.

In early autumn it produces tiny flowers which are nothing to look at, but which fill the air around it with the fragrance of cinnamon.

How to start

Young potted plants and aerial tubers are on sale from specialist nurseries, mostly online, in late autumn or winter. Plants should be kept under cover until after the last frosts of the following spring. Aerial tubers, which are about the size of a chick pea, are planted as if they were seeds, singly in peat-free multipurpose or seed compost in 4 inch (10 cm) pots. Put them in a cold frame, an unheated greenhouse, a bright windowsill in a shed, or just leave them on a step, patio or balcony. You won't see anything happening over the winter; small shoots will show from about April to June.

In future years, Chinese yam is easily propagated by various means: you can replant the top third of a harvested underground tuber, or take cuttings from spring shoots. By far the easiest method is to collect the aerial tubers, which grow plentifully in the leaf axils, as they fall from the vine in autumn, and treat them as described above. It's good to plant more than you actually need, because some of them will probably be lost over winter, drowned by a leaky gutter, swept away in a gale, or dug up by mice.

Growing

New plants are ready to go into their permanent positions after the last spring frost, once they're growing quickly. Give them a sunny position. Because the edible parts – the underground tubers – grow straight downwards to a depth of 2 or 3 feet (61 cm-1 m), I think this vegetable is best grown in big containers, with a capacity of 50 litres or more. A barrel, or even a redundant dustbin (painted, perhaps, to make it look respectable) would do well. That avoids the heavy labour of digging out the yams – instead of going down deep, they'll curl around the bottom of the tub.

You can put the plants straight into the ground though, in which case space them a foot (30 cm) apart in soil that's rich in humus. The ground needs to be moist, but it must also drain well – waterlogging is the only thing that will kill Chinese yam. Dig a hole into which your young plant will fit so that it's at roughly the same level as it was in its pot, refill the soil around the roots and tread it down lightly with your foot. Pour a full watering can's worth of water around the plant to settle the soil around the roots.

Chinese yam needs little or no regular attention. Give it a mulch, a couple of inches (5 cm) deep, of garden compost on planting, and every spring afterwards. Personally, I've never watered or fed mine, but it wouldn't hurt to water it generously during a dry summer, especially in dry soil. If there are a lot of weeds early in the year, remove them; once the vine gets going it'll quickly smother any competition.

The vines can be left to trail over the ground, but that's a bit of a waste of its ornamental potential, and of course would take up more space. It will twine through any nearby bushes or trees, fences, pergolas or trellises. If none of those are available, you could grow it up poles in the same way as runner beans.

Problems

None that I've ever heard of.

Harvest & Storage

Some people eat the aerial tubers as if they were tiny potatoes, but they really are very small and I've never quite had the patience for that. The main crop consists of the two or three underground tubers which each plant produces. These will be ready from late autumn and throughout the winter. I've been growing Chinese yam in Somerset for twenty-odd years and have found it to be entirely hardy, though some reports suggest it may be marginal in the colder areas of the UK – this would be another argument for planting it in containers that could be moved under cover, or at least into a more sheltered position, before the autumn frosts.

The tubers are typically in the form of long sausages, finger-thin at the end attached to the plant and broadening out to wrist-thick at the far end, so they look something like a club in a caveman cartoon. (I mean a club used for thumping, rather than a social club.) The flesh is usually white or cream, the skin often reddish or brown.

These tubers grow larger each year if you don't harvest them, and it'll generally take two or three years of growth for them to reach a useable size. They do sometimes become a bit woody with age, so it's worth experimenting with the gap between planting and harvesting: dig them up for inspection at the end of their first summer, and then again the next year, and so on. If there's enough tuber for a portion, eat it and you'll soon get an idea of what you find is the best harvesting age. Two-year-old tubers rarely disappoint.

If you're growing your cinnamon vine in a tub, you can just tip the whole lot out and take what you want. Harvesting those in the ground involves using a garden spade to dig deeply and carefully (the tubers are quite brittle) right around the plant. If you can't get all the tubers out of the ground without breaking them – and you won't be able to – don't worry: the plant will usually regrow from what's left behind. Replant whatever you don't take in a container or in the ground. It won't always regrow, but more often than not it will.

The yams, even broken ones, last quite well in a fridge, naked in the salad drawer, and will keep for at least a couple of months buried in sand (see Resources, pages 234-5) in a cool shed.

EAT YOUR FRONT GARDEN

Chinese yam (*Dioscorea*) produces large edible tubers

EATING

Chinese yams are used like potatoes: boiled, steamed, baked, fried, roasted. I particularly like them baked, but they're also good steamed and then mashed and served in place of rice with a curry. In chunks or slices they can be included in all the usual savoury dishes in which you'd use a root or tuber, such as stews, curries, and soups. They can be peeled or not, just like potatoes, depending on what you're doing with them.

Their texture is slippery when raw, and floury once cooked. The sweetish flavour is usually described as mild but pleasant. That's true, but it undersells what many people find a quite ambrosial vegetable.

Summer flowers of Caucasian spinach (*Hablitzia*)

Caucasian spinach (*Hablitzia tamnoides*)

Also known as: Hablitzia, Climbing spinach,
Scandinavian spinach.

Vegetable growers of the world owe thanks to the gardening writer Stephen Barstow (see Resources, pages 234-5) for pretty well single-handedly reintroducing us to this valuable crop. It's a hardy, herbaceous, perennial vine, which spreads slowly to form mounded clumps. Originally from the Caucasus, it was known in Britain as an ornamental from the 1820s. Prized as an informal 'pillar plant' for training up garden features such as statuary in grand gardens, it was occasionally grown as a vegetable – particularly in Scandinavia – but subsequently seems to have been forgotten by all but a few gardeners until its revival at the end of the twentieth century.

Ornamental value

Right – bear with me on this… Caucasian spinach is an ornamental. It was originally introduced to this country as an ornamental. In Victorian times, it was grown as an ornamental. It even became mildly fashionable for a time *as an ornamental*. You might say to me, 'But it's not ornamental', to which I will reply, with exaggerated patience, 'No: but it is *an* ornamental'. So you see, you can't sue me: I've covered myself with my cunningly precise use of words.

Tastes change – in ornamental climbers as in all other things – and this slightly untidy plant doesn't really look like something you'd see in a modern garden centre. On the other hand, it doesn't really look like a vegetable, either, so it certainly qualifies for the invisible allotment.

It'll grow to a height of 10 feet (3 m), possibly more, and scramble sideways at the same time for a few feet, so it's good for covering fences or other eyesores. The young green and bronze shoots, a couple of inches tall from late autumn, reminiscent of *Sempervivum* (otherwise known as houseleeks), are attractive, though not very prominent; the heart-shaped green leaves are pleasant enough; the small, green, summer flowers are individually insignificant, but because they are carried in profuse racemes they give a feathery effect when viewed from a short distance.

How to start

Caucasian spinach grows readily from seed, but the seeds aren't widely available – perhaps they will be in the future, if the plant catches on as it deserves to. Sow one or two in a small pot of seed compost in autumn, and leave them exposed to the cold of winter. The seeds are very small, so only lightly cover them with compost. They should germinate in early spring.

A small but increasing number of websites offer divisions of hablitzia in autumn and spring. Hablitzia can be propagated by division of existing clumps in autumn. Dig out a lump from a clump with a spade, and replant it immediately. In spring, you can take a shoot cutting, using a sharp knife to slice off a shoot with a sliver of the crown of the root attached – this can then be potted in a small pot of peat-free multipurpose compost. Or, also in spring, you can slice your knife downwards through the clump to take off a mini-clump of shoots and root, making sure that your new bit has at least one bud on it.

Whichever method you use, grow the new plants on in small

Caucasian spinach (*Hablitzia*) produces edible shoots in winter

pots, under cover or in a sheltered position, for planting out in late spring or early summer once they're growing well.

Growing

Planting out Caucasian spinach is straightforward: tip the new plant out of its pot, slapping the bottom of the pot sharply with a trowel if the rootball is reluctant to come out. Use the trowel to dig a hole in the ground about the same size as the rootball, and settle the plant into it. Firm it down with your hands, and water it thoroughly.

All this rapidly growing climber needs to succeed is a position in full sun or dappled shade, and something to climb up. You could grow it up a house wall on a trellis. I put mine next to a six-foot chain-link fence, and when it runs out of fence it clambers extravagantly into a neighbouring tree.

Easy to grow, hablitzia doesn't need any maintenance. It never seems to need feeding, nor is it fussy about the condition of the soil. Most of its growth occurs, explosively, from early spring to early summer, so it will rarely if ever need watering.

The clumps spread quite slowly from one year to the next.

Problems

None.

Harvest & Storage

Both the shoots and the leaves are eaten – as are the shoots that have begun to produce leaves – and can be taken at any time that they're present.

A well-established clump will produce scores of shoots every year.

As with asparagus, you cut off the tender tips for use and discard any woody lower growth. In my garden, the young, leafless shoots are usually available before Christmas and then right through the winter, making them a very useful vegetable at a time when not much else is showing.

The leafy shoots are around from late winter or early spring. I take the top set of leaves and an inch (2.5 cm) or so of stem from each one. Shoots regrow after cutting, and I'll harvest them two or three times each year before letting them grow on.

Mature leaves follow from late spring throughout the summer; take as many as you need – there'll be plenty.

EATING

The shoots can be used wherever you might use either spinach or asparagus, and the summer leaves as a tastier, drought-resistant alternative to spinach. Hablitzia doesn't need much cooking; a five-minute steam will be plenty. The youngest leaves can be used in salads.

All parts have a slightly salt-and-pepper flavour and a pleasing texture, which stands up well to cooking.

Vine leaves (*Vitis*)

Vine leaves (*Vitis*)

Also known as: Grape leaves.

One of the world's most commonly grown fruiting plants, the grape is a deciduous, woody, hardy perennial climber.

Ornamental value

As well as for their fruit, and the juice of their fruit, grapevines have long been grown for their decorative qualities. Trained up and over a structure – smart, like an arch, or rustic, like a lash-up of poles and wires – they produce a dappled area for summer sitting which has induced a feeling of relaxation in humans for thousands of years. The vines are just as attractive when left to ramble and climb through other plants, their leaves and tendrils appearing here and there through the foliage of their neighbours. From late spring, the young leaves and tendrils look shiny and full of life, a display which culminates in the changing colours of their autumn leaves, which vary according to variety. The size of the plants is also variable, but they'll generally reach about 10 feet (3 m) tall and wide – though that can be controlled by pruning.

How to start

Grapevines can be started from seed, or by taking hardwood cuttings from an existing plant, but by far the easiest and most reliable method (though not the cheapest, obviously) is to buy a young plant from a nursery or garden centre in the autumn.

Any grape will do for leaves, but do have a look through the plant catalogues as some varieties (for instance, Pinot Noir) are sometimes recommended for leaf crops. They also differ in autumnal leaf colour, which might affect your choice. You should also check that the one you fancy is considered fully hardy in your part of the country.

Growing

Grapevines grown for fruit can be quite difficult to get right. If you're only interested in the leaves, however, they are much easier. Vines can be planted at any time they're dormant, from late autumn until the beginning of spring, provided the ground isn't frozen or waterlogged. Remove the plant from its pot, having watered it well the day before, and use your fingers to fan out the roots. Dig a hole in the ground and place the plant in it so that it is at the same level to the soil as it was to the compost in its pot. If you've bought a bare root plant, one that isn't in a pot, you should be able to tell by a tidemark on the stem how deeply it was previously planted. Backfill the soil, firm it around the roots with your boot, and then give a throrough watering to the soil for a couple of feet around the stem. Mulch around the stem with a few inches' depth of chipped bark, old manure or garden compost, to protect the new plant from frost for its first few months. That mulch will need to be scraped back in spring, after the last of the frosts, to prevent it rotting the stem. The spot you've selected for your vine can be in full sun or partial shade. Grapes grow best in deep, rich soil, but they'll do well enough anywhere that doesn't get waterlogged.

If, where you've planted the grape, the soil around its roots is exposed, mulch it every spring to conserve moisture. If the base of the plant is shaded by other plants, this is unlikely to be necessary.

Because we're growing for leaves not fruit, water well in dry weather. Feed the vines occasionally with a liquid fertiliser, such as seaweed solution, only if they seem to need it – generally, they grow vigorously without extra feeding.

I have tried to grow vines in pots, but with what I like to call 'limited success' (i.e. no success at all). Apart from anything, they dry out very quickly, so if you do keep your grape in a container make sure it's a big one – something about the size of a barrel – or be prepared to water it twice a day in the summer.

Pruning on grapevines is mainly done to force the vigorous, fast-growing plants to produce more fruit and fewer leaves. Since we want leaves, not fruit, we don't really have to prune at all. Harvesting the leaves for use is often pruning enough. But while the vines look elegant winding through adjacent shrubs, they can travel quite a long way. At any time during the growing season, when you spot a shoot getting too long, or heading somewhere you don't want it to go, all you need to do is use your thumbnail, or scissors or secateurs, to cut off the leading couple of inches of that shoot. You can cut off much more than that – even whole shoots – if necessary. There's only one thing to remember: if you ever need to do any remedial pruning, cutting into dry wood rather than juicy stems, do it during the winter while the plant is dormant.

For the best crop of leaves, it's easy enough to prevent fruit forming just by snipping off any bunches of the tiny flowers as they appear. If you miss the flowers, you can do the same to the fruit, later on.

Problems

I grow one grape in the back garden for fruit, and one in the front for leaves. In the back garden I get mildew, and lose fruit to birds and wasps and rodents (I always call them rodents rather than rats; I think I find the ambiguity comforting. After all, rodents could mean mice, or it could mean those little furry ones with the long tails that you see on nature programmes. It doesn't have to mean rats. In fact, it means rats, but...)

The front garden vine suffers no problems. Grapes can be prone to fungal diseases, which show up as a powdery coating on leaves and fruit, but this is less likely if there is plenty of air circulation around the foliage.

Harvest & Storage

The main leaf picking time is from late spring to early or mid-summer, when there are masses of tender young leaves. Look for ones that are supple, still light in colour, undamaged, and large enough for your purpose. If you're planning to stuff them, they'll need to be the size of your palm at least. Cut the leaf from the plant at the base of the stem, where the stem joins the vine.

The leaves will keep in a plastic bag in the fridge for a few days. For longer-term storage there are several good options: they freeze well, or they can be dried, they can be stored in airtight pickling jars, or brined. But the simplest way of keeping vine leaves is the plastic bottle method. This sounds too good to be true, yet it really works. Dab each leaf dry with kitchen roll or a clean tea towel, removing any dust or debris, but don't wash them. Work gently, so as not to tear the leaves. Now take about half a dozen leaves at a time, and roll them up like a cigar. Push the cigars down the neck of a dry, clean plastic bottle. Use a small bottle, and stuff it as full as you can, so that there's as little air as possible in it. Screw the cap on, tightly, and put the bottle in a cool, dark cupboard. The leaves should keep for about a year. When you want to use them you cut the bottle open to get them out, use them as if they were fresh, and the bottle can go into the recycling.

EATING

There is a bit more to vine leaves than dolmades – but does there really need to be? I think this wonderfully tasty, satisfying dish – versions of which are found in dozens of countries under many different names – became a standard part of the British diet in the mid-1970s when Cypriot refugees opened restaurants, takeaways and convenience stores. Today you'll find lots of recipes for stuffed vine leaves both online and in cookery books. In their simplest form they are vine leaves wrapped like parcels around dollops of a cooked mixture of rice, tomatoes, onion, herbs and whatever else you fancy, which are then steamed in a dish or pan with a little water until they're tender.

Grape leaves are usually blanched (in the culinary, not the horticultural, sense) before being used. Having cut the stems off, rinse the leaves in cold water. Boil a large pan of water, add the leaves and immediately turn off the heat. Leave the leaves in the water for about three minutes, then fish them out, drain them and use them. Blanched leaves have a lemony tartness and a grapey aroma.

As well as getting stuffed, vine leaves are used to wrap around other foods during cooking. Food steamed or braised on a bed of vines leaves will take on a subtle flavour. Very young leaves are sometimes used in salad.

Larger leaves are extremely useful in pickles and ferments, serving as an inner 'lid' to keep the pickled food from rising above the liquid, and also to keep the contents crisp, because they contain tannin.

Hop shoots (*Humulus*)

Hop shoots (*Humulus lupulus*)

A very hardy, herbaceous perennial, common both as a wild plant and a crop through most of northern Europe, the hop produces winding stems called 'bines', meaning vines that climb without tendrils.

Most of the world's cultivated hops are used in making beer, a practice which arrived in Britain from Europe, against much opposition, during the fifteenth century. Their preservative qualities allowed ale, a homemade staple, to become beer – a commodity. Hops are sometimes raised on allotments and in gardens for use in home-brewing, but only rarely as a vegetable.

Hop shoots are often described, rightly or wrongly, as the world's most expensive vegetable, presumably because to get enough to sell a grower would have to hand-pick hundreds of tiny shoots over a very short period. If you do manage to find them on sale, you'll probably have to pay hundreds of pounds for a kilo. The use of the shoots goes back centuries, but whether or not it predates the use of the flowers in brewing is uncertain.

Ornamental value

The plant lives underground during the winter, reappearing as tiny shoots in spring. During a warm, wet spring they can grow several inches a day, quickly becoming bines. The leaves which grow from them are usually green, though they are also available golden or variegated. Initially heart-shaped, they later divide into three large lobes.

Through spring and early summer the bines grow rapidly

upwards; once the days begin to shorten, at the end of June, they stop growing vertically and start spreading horizontally. It's these side growths that carry the flowers – but only on female plants. The papery, pale green flowers are also known as hops or cones, and they're the part that's used to flavour beer. They form in mid- to late summer. A hop plant with numerous cones hanging among its foliage is a beautiful sight, especially in September when the cones begin to dry and their colours turn autumnal.

A hop plant can reach around 20 feet (6 m) tall, but is easily kept to the size you require just by cutting off any excess growth at any time. Dwarf cultivars tend to be about half the size, and can be grown in large tubs. They can be planted to screen something you don't want to look at (during the summer, anyway), and grown on fences or other garden structures such as rose arches.

How to start

Seeds are sold by a few catalogues and websites. Sow them indoors in early spring or early autumn, somewhere where the temperature is always cool but not frozen: the windowsill in an unused bedroom, an unheated conservatory, or a well-insulated shed or garage. Fill a 3 inch (7.5 cm) pot with moist, peat-free seed compost, put two or three seeds on the surface, and cover them over with about an eighth of an inch (3 mm) of the same compost. Hop seeds can be slow and erratic in their germination, but by early spring you should have small plants ready for planting out.

I started with seeds, and more than twenty years later my plants are still doing fine, producing shoots and flowers. But to make sure you get a female plant – and to have more choice in cone size, foliage colour and the growth habit of the plant – you can buy a named type from an online nursery. They're usually available as bare root plants from midwinter to mid-spring, and some places sell them as young plants in pots from late spring to midwinter.

The easiest way to make new hop plants from an existing one is layering. Any time in spring, when the bines are growing well, select a shoot that is long enough to be bent down to ground level without breaking, and which has three or four sets of leaves on it. Remove one set of leaves from the middle of the shoot. Fill a 6 inch (15 cm) pot with soil or with peat-free multipurpose compost, and bury a few inches of the leafless stretch of the bine in the pot, about an inch and a half (4 cm) deep – without removing the shoot from the plant. Use a piece of U-shaped bent wire as a peg to prevent the bine from rising up out of the compost. Leave the pot there, watering to make sure it never dries out, until the following spring, by which time a new plant should have grown in the pot, which can now have its connection to the parent plant severed and be planted out on its own.

GROWING

Plants bought as bare roots should be planted as soon as they arrive. Those in pots should be put in their final position in November or December. Choose a sunny position, preferably in rich, moist soil (though once they're established, because of their deep roots, they are resistant to drought). Try not to expose hops to too much wind, as that might make it harder for them to climb. Dig a hole so that when you put the plant in it's a couple of inches (5 cm) below the level of the soil. Refill the hole, firm the soil down with your boot, and water thoroughly. Surround the plant with a mulch of compost or manure, and repeat that every spring. Each plant will need about 3 feet (1 m) of ground between it and neighbouring plants. You won't see much in the first year – possibly two – while the plant establishes itself.

Hops need something to cling to. They'll use nearby shrubs or trees, but might smother them, so it's best to give them their own support. Fences, arches, poles, wires or strings will all do the job. Pruning is straightforward: every spring cut all last year's growth right back to the ground.

When working on hops, note that the bines, and the undersides of the leaves, are scratchy and can irritate the skin, so wear gloves and long sleeves.

Problems

The pests and diseases seen in commercial hop fields rarely occur in gardens, when you're only growing one or two plants.

The only serious problem I've ever had with hops is due to the tendency of the woody root system to travel underground for several yards. I put mine next to a patio, and every year I have to try and dig out roots and rhizomes which pop up in gaps between the flagstones. Make sure you position yours so that it will only run in open soil, where you can get at it.

Harvest & Storage

The shoots are taken in April and May – traditionally, they were a bonus vegetable for the workers pruning commercial hop fields in spring. Cut them off close to the ground when they're 4-6 inches (10-15 cm) long. The top 3-4 inches (7.5-10 cm) of side shoots produced during the summer are also edible. Always let some shoots grow on, so as to maintain the plant as a perennial. Established hop plants will produce a lot of shoots, but 'a lot' is relative; you're never going to get a glut of a vegetable which is, individually, so small.

Shoots will keep in a plastic bag in the fridge for a few days, but they're usually used fresh – they're not worth freezing. They are sometimes pickled.

A popular non-food use for hops is to cut lengths of bine with cones on in September, for hanging in the house as an aromatic decoration; they'll gradually dry in situ. The scent of autumn hops is my earliest memory, but even people who weren't born in Kent usually find it a wonderful smell.

Eating

Hop shoots are most often eaten as if they were miniature asparagus spears, steamed or boiled for three or four minutes until they're tender. Another traditional method is to boil the stems in a little broth or stock, and then serve them on hot, buttered toast. They can be steamed and then fried, or chopped and used as the green herb in a buttery or creamy sauce – in place of, for instance, parsley or chives – or in soups, omelettes, and salads.

The flavour is something like asparagus, with a bitterness like chicory, and a slight nuttiness. If you find the shoots too bitter, next time try soaking them in salted water for an hour before cooking.

Some people eat other parts of the plant. Young leaves are occasionally used in salad, and larger leaves as dolmades, like vine leaves (see pages 171-5). The petals of the cones are sometimes used in cooking, but very sparingly.

Nasturtium (*Tropaeolum majus*)

SECTION FOUR

PLANTS GROWN MAINLY FOR GROUND COVER

Crosnes (*Stachys*) used as ground cover

CROSNES (*STACHYS AFFINIS*)

Also known as: Chinese artichoke, Chorogi, Knot root.

This hardy herbaceous perennial, native to China and Japan, was introduced to Europe in the 1880s, hence the French name: Crosne is a place near Paris. It was popular for a few years, but fell out of fashion after the Great War – possibly because it is a fiddly vegetable if used in quantity, and there was no longer a ready supply of cheap labour to sieve crosne out of the winter soil in the garden, or scrub their twirly crevices clean in the kitchen.

ORNAMENTAL VALUE

The genus *Stachys* is in the same family as mint, and you can tell that from the small, fuzzy, crinkled green leaves and upright stems. The foliage, from very early spring to autumn, grows to about 18 inches (46 cm) tall, with a spread of about 12 inches (30 cm). A patch of crosnes will spread quite quickly, making a useful, if unspectacular ground cover.

Spikes of quite pleasant pink flowers often appear in mid-summer, which are attractive to bees and which can be cut for vases.

HOW TO START

You can buy young plants at the start of spring, but save your money – Chinese artichokes will grow just as quickly from tubers, which are sold by many seed catalogues and online suppliers. Order them from around Christmas time, and plant them as soon as they arrive. If the ground's too frozen or soggy to work on, then plant each tuber in a small pot of peat-free multipurpose compost and leave the pot outside for planting in the spring.

Growing

Make small holes in the soil with a dibber, or your finger, and drop a tuber in, so that it's covered by an inch (2.5 cm) or so of soil. A precise planting depth doesn't seem to be important, nor does whether the tuber goes in upright or sideways. Space them 6 inches (15 cm) apart for the quickest ground cover, or 12 inches (30 cm) apart for the biggest tubers. Or, I suppose, 9 inches (23 cm) apart if you can't decide.

Position Chinese artichokes in full sun for the biggest yield of tubers, but they will also grow in shade, and they'll tolerate most soils, though they do best in rich, sandy ground. Good drainage is important for overwintering; they are untroubled by low temperatures, but I have lost a bed of them in wet soil following a thaw.

It's most practical to grow them in the same place permanently, because it's impossible to be sure that you've harvested every last tuber so the patch will tend to persist whether you want it to or not. In containers, you're unlikely to get such a big crop but it's still worthwhile and has the advantage that the tubers come out much cleaner.

Crosnes doesn't recover well from drying out: its foliage goes floppy, and the plant becomes dormant, so it needs attentive watering during hot weather. A liquid feed could be beneficial in high summer.

Crosnes don't seem to suffer much from overcrowding, which means you can leave the bed largely to fend for itself, harvesting whenever you feel like it in the winter, or not bothering if you don't get round to it. Thinning the plants out might produce slightly larger tubers, but I can't believe the gain would be worth the effort. Some people earth up the stems when the flowers are a foot tall in summer, by piling soil or compost around them to a depth of a few inches, to encourage tuber formation. I've never noticed any difference when I've done this, but it's perhaps worth a go.

PROBLEMS

None.

HARVEST & STORAGE

When the foliage is killed by autumn frosts, use a hand fork to dig out the tubers. They grow in strings, are ivory white, and usually an inch or two (2.5-5 cm) long, and half an inch (12.5 mm) wide. They're segmented, and I would suggest it's impossible to look at them without being reminded of the larval stage of large beetles. Yields are rarely generous, but a small patch of crosnes should give you enough for a couple of meals.

The tubers don't store at all well – they dehydrate quickly, discolour and become limp – which must be one reason why they're rarely seen for sale in shops. However, they can safely be left in the ground for harvest when needed. When the foliage is dead, cover the soil with a mulch of autumn leaves or straw, or even newspaper or office shreddings. The mulch will freeze solid, and

Crosnes (*Stachys*) tubers

you can then lift it off like a lid to get at the unfrozen soil beneath. Tubers mostly grow near the surface, so there's no need to dig deep when harvesting, unless you're trying to get rid of them.

In theory, you could keep some of the tubers you harvest for replanting the following year, but I've never known this to be necessary. There will always be a few left behind, from which the patch will regrow.

EATING

Even when lightly cooked, the tubers have a crunchy texture like radish or water chestnut. The flavour is sweet when raw, and more starchy when cooked. They do taste something like a nuttier version of artichoke, although they have no botanical connection to actual artichokes.

Crosnes don't need peeling – the skin is very thin – but they do need washing, and depending on your soil that can be tiresome: their shape makes them good at trapping dirt, and their smallness means they're difficult to scrub. The key thing is to get them into a bowl of cold water for ten minutes or so immediately after lifting them. That soaking will get rid of most of the mud, and agitating them around in the water with your fingers should dislodge the rest. If you're really having trouble, try this: put the tubers in the middle of a tea towel, sprinkle a good handful of salt over them, then close the towel over them and rub them vigorously within it for a couple of minutes, and then rinse them in a sieve.

In Japan they're mostly used for short-term pickles, or longer-term ferments, often with the addition of perilla (see pages 93-7) for colouring. They can be eaten raw, added without prior cooking to soups, stir-fries and casseroles, or parboiled and then fried. To cook, steam or boil them for about four minutes – at that stage, you can use them in salads, adding the dressing while they're still warm.

Nasturtium (*Tropaeolum majus*)

Nasturtium (*Tropaeolum majus*)

Also known as: Indian cress.

This half-hardy annual is, of course, an extremely familiar garden plant and a rather obvious choice for this book. But it would be daft to leave it out, as it is surely the most entirely edible and useful flower you can possibly grow in Britain. The genus *Tropaeolum* is thought to have originated in the Americas, being introduced to Europe in the sixteenth century, principally for use in salads.

Ornamental value

Nasturtium is available in dwarf and trailing forms, so some make low-growing mounds, while others sprawl, ramble and climb energetically along the ground, through shrubs, up fences and into trees. They are used in the garden both as climbers and as a weed-suppressing ground cover that will rapidly occupy bare patches between other plants. They also look good tumbling from hanging baskets.

The thin, rounded leaves are usually green, but there are also variegated types. Drops of dew or rain sit on them, sparkling in the sun. As they get older in autumn and start turning yellow, their veins become more visible and they'll often take on patterns that look like giant snowflakes. Even while that's happening, there will still be some new young growth coming elsewhere in the nasturtium patch.

The prolific, quite large, normally five-petalled flowers come in various shades of red, orange, cream and yellow, and are intensely attractive to many insects, especially bumblebees and hoverflies. They make good, though not long-lived, cut flowers. They are slightly fragrant.

How to start

If you're in a hurry, you don't really need to sow nasturtiums: just buy a packet of seeds, chuck a handful of them around your garden one spring, and the seedlings will pop up here and there within a few weeks. Self-sown plants will appear randomly for years to come. If they grow anywhere you don't want them to, they're no trouble to pull up.

For greater precision, sow directly into the soil any time in spring by pushing the large seeds into the ground to a depth of about half an inch (12.5 mm). They can also be started under cover from March, singly in 3 inch (7.5 cm) pots, in peat-free seed or multipurpose compost, for planting out in early summer.

Growing

Part of the reason for the nasturtium's popularity, along with its beauty and utility, is that it is so easy to grow. It'll take to any non-waterlogged soil, and is therefore useful for filling in areas of poor ground. For maximum leaf production, choose rich, moist soil; for maximum flowers and seeds, thinner, drier soil. But in practice, you'll get plenty of all three elements wherever you grow it. The flowers do best in full sun, but nasturtium will also be fine in partial shade.

Indian cress never needs feeding or watering, or indeed any attention at all. The only exception is if you're growing it in containers (it'll do well in any container, of any size from about

5 inches (13 cm) upwards) when it might be in danger of drying out during hot weather.

I've noticed over the years that nasturtiums in different parts of my garden die off from frosts at varying rates – one patch will be killed by the first frost of the autumn, while another, just a yard or so away, will survive for another week or two. If you know which spots in your garden are most sheltered from frosts, you might want to put your plants there.

PROBLEMS

Because they grow so enthusiastically, nasturtiums can swamp other plants. If they behave like weeds, treat them as weeds, and just pull up as much as you need to.

Sometimes grown as 'sacrificial plants', to draw pests away from cabbages and the like, nasturtiums are very attractive to blackfly and to the caterpillars of white butterflies. There's not much you can do about this – unless you're willing to spray poisons around your garden – but even if some leaves are ruined, I always find that others replace them once the lifecycle of the creature responsible has moved on to its next phase.

HARVEST & STORAGE

The flowers, seed pods, leaves and stems are all edible, and all are produced in great numbers.

The foliage is present from late spring or early summer until the plant is killed by frost in the autumn. Younger, smaller leaves tend to have a more pleasant texture and subtler flavour than older ones. They can be harvested at any time, provided you leave plenty on each plant for it to continue growing. Flowers are there all summer, from early June in my garden, and can be picked freely. I take the seed pods, which grow in clumps of three on the end of long stalks beneath the foliage, from July or August, until about October.

Flowers and leaves can be dehydrated for use as flavouring in cooked dishes, and the leaves can be frozen as a green veg. Leaves and seeds will keep in a plastic bag in the fridge for two or three days, and flowers in a glass jar in the fridge for four or five days, but really, all parts are better used straight away.

The best-known way of preserving nasturtium is to pickle the seed pods. The traditional name for these is 'poor man's capers', but there's nothing poor about them – they are delicious. You'll find lots of recipes for nasturtium capers in books, magazines, and on the internet, and they all produce slightly different results. To get you started, here's the one I use.

Select light green pods, which don't yet feel hard (once their colour starts to turn slightly reddish or grey, they're past their best). Pick them on a dry day, and avoid washing them if possible: any water clinging to them could make the brining process less effective.

Dissolve two ounces of salt in a pint of cold water to make brine. Put the pods into a bowl, and cover with the brine. Leave the bowl somewhere reasonably cool and dark for 24 hours. Drain the pods through a sieve, discarding the brine. Don't rinse them.

Prepare some small glass jars by washing them in hot soapy water, and rinsing them in hot clean water. Put them in an oven, pre-heated to 275 °F / 140 °C / Gas Mark 1, for around ten minutes until they're thoroughly dry. You can use special preserving jars – the 'terrine' size is best – but jam or pickle jars that aren't chipped or cracked, and have plastic-lined lids, will do fine. To get the size of jar right, I take it with me when I'm picking the pods, and fill it with them so that there's a headspace of about half an inch (12.5 mm).

When the jars have completely cooled, pack the seed pods into them and fill to the top with malt vinegar, straight from the bottle. Put the lids on, and store the capers in a cool, dark, dry cupboard. They'll be ready to eat in three months, and will keep, unopened, for a year.

Eating

All the edible parts of the nasturtium have a good, peppery flavour, like watercress, to varying degrees. In addition to that, the flowers have a slight taste of honey.

The leaves are eaten raw in salads and sandwiches, steamed as a green vegetable, stuffed, used in place of basil in making pesto or in place of watercress in soup, and added as an ingredient to pasta and rice dishes, especially risotto.

The flowers are also good in salads and sandwiches, as an ingredient in rice and pasta recipes, as a receptacle or wrap for dips and patés, and as a garnish to any dish, hot or cold. The seeds are sometimes put in salads, but their flavour raw is a bit brutal, and they can have a drying effect on the mouth. They are good in soups, though.

As for the capers, they are perfect as the accompaniment to cheese or to any fatty food, and they're also used in salads, and as a transformative topping for a takeaway pizza.

Oca (*Oxalis*) as ground cover

Oca (*Oxalis tuberosa*)

Also known as: New Zealand yam.

A bushy, tender perennial, in temperate regions like ours oca is usually grown as an annual, with tubers kept back for replanting. Even more so than mashua (see pages 139-49) this is one of the main tuberous crops of the traditional Andean diet. In Britain, it was grown in the nineteenth century as an ornamental, but is now being revived as an allotment vegetable. It's been raised as a crop in New Zealand since the nineteenth century.

Ornamental value

From spring to autumn, oca forms a mound of clover-like leaves growing on fleshy stems. The foliage is light green, sometimes with a tinge of gold. Quite neat in habit, each plant will grow to about 18 inches (46 cm) tall and 2 feet (61 cm) across. It forms an excellent ground cover, smothering weeds and keeping the soil moist while looking attractive, kempt and somewhat exotic.

Under certain conditions ocas sometimes produce buttercup-like flowers in mid-summer.

How to start

Today, oca tubers are quite widely sold in spring by large mail order seed companies, as well as specialist websites. In fact, UK seed companies are increasingly offering a choice of varieties, with tubers in various shades of red, yellow, cream, pink, scarlet and purple.

When your tubers arrive, 'chit' them just as you would with seed potatoes – in other words, lay them on a tray in a cool, light, frost-free place such as a windowsill in an unheated room. Over the next couple of weeks colourful shoots will sprout from their sides. At that point, they are ready to be planted. If you're already past the date when you expect the last frost in your area, then you could plant them straight into the garden. If not, put them about 3 inches (7.5 cm) deep, individually, in peat-free multipurpose compost in 5 inch (13 cm) pots, and keep them somewhere light and safe from frost for planting out in late spring or early summer. I put mine in a plastic mini-greenhouse. If oca are damaged by frost they'll generally recover, though they'll have lost some of their limited growing time.

In future years, save a few tubers at harvest time for use as next year's 'seed'. Pick the largest to keep back, making sure they're in good condition. Put them in a paper bag, and keep them in a cool room or a cool cupboard, in darkness. If you live in a place with an old-fashioned larder, that would be exactly right. From January onwards, check the saved tubers every week. Soon, probably in February or March, they will start sprouting. If you leave them in the dark, their shoots will become long, tangled and brittle, so now's the time to chit the tubers as described above.

Outside its native range oca does not carry viruses from one generation to the next, unlike potatoes, so you can re-use your own tubers as seed stock indefinitely.

GROWING

Whether you're planting tubers directly into the soil, or using small plants that you've started in pots, space them 12-18 inches

(30-46 cm) apart, in a sunny position. I like to plant them at a depth where the sprouting shoots – or the foliage if the plant is that advanced – are mostly covered by soil. I couldn't swear this makes a difference to growth, but I feel it at least provides some protection to the shoots from getting snapped off, and the leaves from unforecast frost.

Oca doesn't do so well in heavy clay soils, and will die in cold, wet soil. Its preference is for light, well-fed ground. Fork a bucketful of garden compost or old manure into the soil before planting. In early summer, mulch around the plants with garden compost (home-made, or bought in bags from a garden centre). Oca needs plenty of moisture to form good tubers, so water the plants at ground level whenever the weather is dry, remembering to carry on doing so in autumn, which is when the tubers are swelling. During very hot weather the leaves will fold up in daytime (something they normally do at night) to conserve moisture – a useful signal that extra watering might be needed.

Whether or not you should earth up ocas, as you do with potatoes, by piling soil around the stems is a matter of debate – some say this increases the yield, others that it produces more tubers but of smaller size. My own experiments have been inconclusive (especially the first year, when I forgot to weigh the subsequent crop). If you have the space and the inclination, it would be worth trying both approaches.

Oca grows well in containers of peat-free multipurpose compost, but they do need a great deal of watering. The pots don't need to be particularly deep, though a diameter of more than 12 inches (30 cm) seems to work best, and the larger the tub, the more slowly the compost will dry out. Oca also looks good in low-level wall baskets.

Problems

I've never heard of oca getting any disease in this country, a great advantage it has over potatoes. It's much less troubled by slugs and wireworms than the potato, too. I've only ever had one serious pest problem, and that only for one year. That winter, when I harvested my pots of oca, I found very few tubers, and in the compost there were small, white grubs, which might have been the larvae of vine weevil. It's never happened again, so I think perhaps the grubs were already present in the compost from a previous crop. I always reuse compost, because it's so expensive, but I don't suppose it's really best practice.

In the comparatively mild climate of Somerset, I find that oca often 'volunteers', the way potatoes do – i.e. small tubers survive in the ground over the winter and come up again in the spring. It doesn't cause me any difficulties because the plants are easy to spot and easy to pull out if they're in the wrong place.

Harvest & Storage

Like mashua, this plant is day-length dependent – meaning that it doesn't form tubers until after mid-summer when, in our part of the world, the frosts are only a few weeks away. The tubers will never be ready for harvest before November at the earliest, so to grow oca for tubers in Britain what we need is a long, frost-free autumn. If your ocas are in pots, of course, you can put them under cover, in a greenhouse or cold frame for instance, before the weather turns. Those in the ground should be covered by glass or plastic cloches, or thick horticultural fleece, if an early frost is forecast.

However, you don't need to worry about the first freeze of autumn – unless it's a freakishly heavy one. Once the leaves have

A harvest of oca (*Oxalis*) tubers

been killed, leave the plants for at least another couple of weeks if you can; there is evidence that the tubers continue to increase in size during this period. It's only when subsequent frosts turn the foliage completely mushy that you need to harvest. Where I live this happens any time from November to January.

In the open ground, lift the whole clump of oca out with a garden fork. Plants grown in containers can be tipped out. If some tubers are still attached to the plant, snip them off with scissors or secateurs. Rub off any excessive soil or compost, and put the tubers on a tray or in a basket, indoors, for a week so that any soil still clinging to them dries out. Don't be too quick to throw away any damaged tubers – if they're not actually rotting they will still keep for a few weeks, and with the damage cut out will be perfectly edible. The size of the smooth, shiny tubers varies a lot, but the most common range is from an inch (2.5 cm) to 6 inches (15 cm) long, and an inch (2.5 cm) across.

Store the tubers you're planning to eat in exactly the same way as described earlier for the ones you're keeping for replanting – but keep the eaters and planters separately, and carefully labelled in large writing, because *certain people* have been known to use the planters for cooking. Oca tubers keep very well for several months until they start regrowing in late winter or early spring, their waxy skins preventing them from drying out. Even if they do shrivel a bit, neither their edibility nor their suitability for replanting will be impaired.

In this country, you can't expect big crops comparable to potatoes – a pound (half a kilo) per plant would be a very respectable result.

Eating

If you treat oca, with its dense, white flesh, as if it were a waxy new potato its use in the kitchen becomes obvious. It's excellent in a potato salad, for instance, or parboiled and then fried or roasted. Added whole to stews, curries and soups the tubers keep their shape and the slow cooking gives them a perfect combination of firm outside and soft inside texture, with an intense carroty, almost orangey, flavour. There's also a tang, similar to sorrel, from oxalic acid. In storage, the acidity reduces and the fruity sweetness increases – if you find them too acidic, expose the tubers to sunlight for a week.

They can be eaten raw, but I think they have much more flavour cooked. Oca is never peeled, by the way, and the shiny skin means that they are the easiest vegetable to wash that I've ever grown.

Hosta grows best in light shade

Hosta (*Hosta*)

Also known as: Plantain lilies, Urui, Giboshi.

There are more than forty species, and thousands of cultivars, in this genus of completely hardy, clump-forming, herbaceous perennials. They grow best in shade, which goes a long way to explaining their great popularity in British gardens – if you've got a shady, moist patch of ground where nothing succeeds but weeds, hosta will fill it, brighten it up, and smother the weeds. Hosta is used as a vegetable in some East Asian countries, especially Japan where it is raised as a commercial crop.

Ornamental value

Grown primarily for its large, usually heart-shaped leaves, which are present from early to mid-spring until early to mid-autumn, hosta is available in many variations of foliage colour, shape and size. You can choose from green, blue, grey, yellow, and variegated.

In June or July, racemes of flowers appear, sometimes scented, on stiff stems which are sometimes 2 to 3 feet (61 cm to 1 m) tall. The attractive, funnel-shaped blooms are usually purple, white, or mauve. Mine last for a fortnight or so, and the bees make good use of them.

How to start

While it is commonly assumed that all hostas are edible, there doesn't seem to be any confident unanimity on the subject. However, there are certain species and cultivars which have either been long used for food, or have been bred for that purpose. Amongst the species most frequently recommended are *H. sieboldiana, H. montana, H. fortunei*, and *H. fluctuans*. Two cultivars which are often nominated as eaters, and which are widely available in the UK as ornamentals, are *H. sieboldiana* 'Elegans', and *H. fluctuans* 'Sagae'. The latter, with its yellow-margined leaves, is my favourite hosta both for eating as well as for looking at.

To start a collection of hostas cheaply, buy a packet of mixed seed, sold in several of the major catalogues. There are two disadvantages to starting from seed: you can't buy particular cultivars, and you'll have to wait a couple of years longer to eat the plants while they get up to size. Seeds are sown at the end of winter or at the start of spring, in trays or pots of seed compost. Just cover the seeds with their own depth in compost, water the trays, and keep them at a temperature of about 50 °F (10 °C). Seedlings should appear within four or five weeks.

Existing plants are easily propagated by division in early autumn or mid-spring. Lift the clump out of the ground with a garden fork, or gently tip it out of its container. Slice the clump into parts using a sharp spade, a knife or a saw, or pull it apart with your hands, depending on how tough the roots are. Make sure each division has four or five shoots on it. Replant both bits, taking care that they go back in at the same depth they were before. Give them a good watering.

The simplest way to start with hostas is to buy young plants in autumn or early spring, either from online sources or from nurseries and garden centres. It'll cost you more, but you will have a wide, not to say bewildering, choice of cultivars.

Growing

Plants and seedlings will be ready to go outside around the end of May, when the ground is warm and there's no likelihood of further spring frosts. As ever, plant them in the ground at the same depth as they were in their pots – any shoots showing should be only just peeping through the surface of the soil. Each plant needs at least 18 inches (46 cm) of space between it and its neighbours.

They'll be at their best in light or medium shade, though they will also grow in full sun or heavy shade. Ideally, the soil should be moisture retentive but with good drainage, and reasonably fertile with lots of compost or manure in it. But hostas are amazingly hard to fail with, so really, just put them wherever you want them.

To give young plants a good start, away from slugs and snails, rather than planting them directly into their final positions, I usually pot them up in 10 litre plastic pots, in peat-free multipurpose compost, and place them on a patio, drive, or other hard-standing area, using pot feet to raise the containers off the ground so as to further foil the slugs, and improve drainage. I do that in October so the hostas have got the rest of the autumn and then the early spring – both relatively slugless seasons – to get established.

The following year in spring or autumn I'll plant them into their final homes, either in bigger pots or in the ground. I tend to prefer autumn planting to spring because the molluscs are on their way into, rather than out of, comparative dormancy, and because the ground is still warm from the summer, albeit cooling, rather than cold from the winter, albeit warming. If you live somewhere with early, hard autumns, that approach might not work for you.

Hosta clumps will spread slowly for about five years (more or less, depending on the type you're growing), and it's likely to be several years after that before you have any need to divide them to prevent overcrowding. Never let them get dry, watering if necessary in hot weather, and every spring mulch the plant heavily with garden compost or a bought-in mulch.

Whenever a hosta seems to have slowed down and lost some of its vigour, instead of feeding it try giving it a thorough weeding and watering first. Only if it hasn't responded to that treatment within a week, feed it with a general purpose liquid fertiliser.

Growing hostas in tubs involves a bit more work, just because they will need more frequent watering and are quite likely to want a liquid feed every month or so. You don't have to give them very big pots – in fact, almost any size that the plant will fit into will do – but remember that the smaller the pot, the sooner you'll need to move the hosta on to a larger size. Peat-free multipurpose compost will suit them fine, but it will need refreshing: every spring, top up the container with new compost. If the tub is so full that you can't top up, then scrape away an inch (2.5 cm) or so of the existing top layer of compost – if you can do so without damaging the plant's roots – and replace it with new.

As the foliage dies in autumn or early winter, pull it off and compost it. When the flowers die, cut off the stems, and compost those too.

Problems

Even if you've never grown a hosta, or even seen one, let alone eaten one, if you've heard of them at all you'll probably know one thing about them – slugs and snails love them. There's no point denying it; hostas are almost proverbially vulnerable to mollusc attack. But even if yours is a particularly sluggy garden, there is quite a lot you can do to reduce this problem.

One reason for growing hostas in sun, despite their preference for shade, is that it's less convenient for molluscs, which move about more easily in darker, cooler sites. If your plants get eaten when they're in the ground, try growing them in tall pots, raised up on bricks or pot feet, so molluscs have to travel across unhospitable plastic or clay to get at them. Bigger cultivars (*H. sibeoldiana* 'Big Daddy' is often mentioned in this context) will grow quicker and more robustly and therefore tend to leave the slugs behind, and some hostas just seem to be less susceptible anyway. Mulching around the plants with gravel, grit, pebbles (or in my case a big bag of glass marbles, which I'd dragged around with me from home to home since childhood and never quite found a use for) will deter molluscs as well as helping to keep the soil moist. I also encircle the plants with copper Slug Rings (http://slugrings.co.uk) which double as enclosures to keep the marbles, or other mulch, in position.

Above all, if you have a lot of trouble with slugs and/or snails, try to grow the hostas as islands surrounded by seas of bare soil. I've experimented with this, and the results are quite startling; those of my hostas which have the foliage of other plants near them (including overhanging them) will get eaten, whereas those which haven't never do. Hoeing the surrounding soil regularly to create a dry, dusty layer on top can help, and obviously rigorous weeding is of the utmost importance.

Deer and rabbits apparently find hostas irresistible as well. I don't get deer or rabbits in my front garden, only dogs, cats and toddlers, but if you do, then…well, possibly hostas aren't for you after all.

HARVEST & STORAGE

Let the plants gather themselves for the first year after planting. Indeed, if at the end of their first settling-in year they don't look very lively and aren't producing many edible shoots, give them another year before you start harvesting. It's worth the wait, because provided they get well established, hostas should live for many years – at least a decade.

Once they're growing strongly you can harvest all the first flush of shoots every spring. Stephen Barstow, one of our most adventurous gardening writers (see Resources, pages 234-5), calls the edible part of hostas 'hostons', because of their resemblance to the chicons of chicory, but I've also seen them called 'quills'. These rolled-up cones of leaves appear any time from March to May, emerging from the bare soil slightly curved, as if they were the horns of a small but colourful beast awakening from its subterranean slumbers. They're very beautiful at this stage, a joyous sight at the end of a long winter.

To harvest the hostons, slice them off at soil level when they're about 6 inches (15 cm) high. The plant will replace them; leave these replacements to grow on. They'll do that pretty quickly, unfurling after a few days from their cigar-shaped rolls into the familiar, broad leaves. You'll be able to tell which ones you've already had a go at, because the new growth will come up from the middle of the harvested shoot.

By growing different hostas, and in different levels of sun and shade, you can stagger your harvest over several weeks.

The hostons will keep in a plastic bag in the fridge for a few days, and in a Green Bag (see Resources, pages 234-5) for a week or two. In Japan they apparently both pickle and dehydrate hosta for out of season use, but I've yet to try either method.

EATING

The juicy, crisp hostons can be eaten raw as salad, but are usually lightly cooked – sautéed, boiled or steamed – as a side dish. I like them steamed for about eight minutes, then served as they are with salt and pepper. They keep their texture well, and the flavour (as

A hosta shoot ready to be cut for eating

with most foods harvested as springs shoots) is very reminiscent of asparagus. The taste is subtle, so they go well with soy sauce, chilli, strongly flavoured cooking oils, lemon juice, and so on.

In Japan they are also used in sushi and tempura recipes. Cut into inches, they can be included in soups, risottos, and scrambled eggs. The later, unfurled, leaves can also be eaten, as general purpose greens or as a spinach substitute. They're very good in lasagne.

By the way, hostas used to belong to a genus called *Funkia*, and the fact that they no longer do is really the only disappointing thing about them.

Fruit of Honeyberry (*Lonicera*)

SECTION FIVE

PLANTS GROWN MAINLY AS HEDGING

Flowers of Japanese quince (*Chaenomeles*) are extremely attractive to bumblebees

Japanese quince (*Chaenomeles*)

Also known as: Flowering quince, Japonica, Mock quince,
Chaenomeles, Maule's quince.

This is not the true quince (*Cydonia oblonga*), which is harder to grow and less commonly seen in gardens, but a genus of three species (and some hybrids) of hardy deciduous shrubs, which are usually spiny.

Ornamental value

The various species, cultivars and hybrids of chaenomeles come in different heights, from forms used as ground cover, at about 2 feet (61 cm) tall, to those that get to 6 feet (2 m) or more. They are frequently used in gardens and parks in Britain as impenetrable hedges, or trained against a wall. It's their glorious flowers that make them so popular – masses of deep red (sometimes orange or white) cup-shaped blooms, generally between February/March and April/May, 1-2 inches (2.5-5 cm) across, with five petals. There are few better sights in early spring.

The glossy, oval, small, dark green leaves in spring and summer are also attractive, as are the autumn fruit, which are the size and shape of small apples (or pears, in some types), around 2 inches (5 cm) across, mostly golden when ripe, but sometimes green or purplish.

Bees enthusiastically visit the early flowers, and small birds roost and sing within the shelter of the spiny branches.

How to start

Young plants are available from almost any nursery, garden centre or website. There's a wide choice in size of shrub and colour of flower, so read the descriptions to find one that fits your plans. They seem to be on sale for most of the year, though the professional consensus has always been that shrubs should be planted either in the autumn or the spring.

Growing

A sunny position is necessary for maximum flower and fruit, but the chaenomeles will tolerate some shade. Any soil with decent drainage and reasonable fertility will suit.

Dig a hole in the ground a little larger than the rootball of the plant. If the plant has arrived in a pot, tap the bottom of the pot to loosen the rootball so you can gently slide it out without too much disturbance to the soil around the roots. Put the plant in the hole so that it sits in contact with the ground, and is at the same depth as it was in the pot – or, if it didn't come in a pot, level it using the mark you can see on the stem showing how deeply it was previously buried. Backfill the hole with the soil you've dug out, firming it down as you go with your boot. Water around the roots to settle the soil. Spread a couple of buckets full of compost for a foot (30 cm) or so around the planting site.

In dry weather you might need to water the new plant until it's established, but other than that the only maintenance you'll ever need to do is pruning – once chaenomeles is growing well it'll never need feeding or watering.

The purpose of pruning is to keep this fast-growing, spiny plant in bounds by cutting back branches that grow into spaces where

EAT YOUR FRONT GARDEN

you don't want them. Chaenomeles is best pruned in about May, just after it finishes flowering. The trouble with that plan is that some chaenomeles, including the one in my front garden, grow so much during the spring and summer that they need to be pruned more than once, and I have also known it to repeat its flowering in summer. In practice, I prune it whenever I have to – i.e. whenever it's getting out of control – and hope for the best.

Problems

There are a few pests and diseases which theoretically can affect mock quince, but in normal garden culture I think they're too rare to worry about. The biggest problem you're likely to encounter with the mock quince comes from putting it in the wrong spot in the first place – or not realising how much it will spread over the years. Mine is right next to the path, and I am always having to hack it back, often at the cost of flowers and fruit, just so that the postman can reach the front door without having his uniform ripped to shreds. You might think this was a stupid mistake to make, but in my defence I would merely point out that, yes, it was – so don't you make it. Luckily, even the most violent assault on a chaenomeles with a cordless hedge trimmer doesn't seem to do any lasting damage.

Harvest & Storage

The fruits will colour in late autumn; leave them where they are (on the bush or on the ground) until there've been one or two frosts, which intensify the flavour. Quinces which have dropped off, or are growing on the outside of the shrub, are easily harvested, but picking those that have grown within the tangle of thorny branches requires either thick gauntlets or great dexterity.

Aromatic fruit of the Japanese quince (*Chaenomeles*)

EATING

You wouldn't want to eat mock quinces raw – they're rock hard, and so astringent they'd pucker your mouth to a point where it might actually vanish altogether.

Instead, they are cooked until soft and then used to make jellies, fruit cheeses, liqueurs, and marmalades (or added to mixed fruit jams). They also go well with apples as a stewed fruit. Jam makers in particular will be pleased to hear that chaenomeles is exceptionally high in pectin.

Broadly speaking, mock quinces can substitute for real quinces in any recipe. Opinion regarding the flavour of *Chaenomeles* ranges from those who find it indistinguishable from *Cydonia*, to others who feel it's inferior. Treated purely on its own merits, however, it is a gorgeous fruit, aromatic, and both sharp and sweet.

If you don't get round to eating the fruits, there's no need to waste them: put them in a bowl or basket in a warm room, and for several weeks their unique, subtle, irresistible perfume will spread throughout your home without ever becoming intrusive. No matter how much you spend, you'll never buy a reed diffuser half so pleasing.

Flowers and hairy leaves of Honeyberry (*Lonicera*)

Honeyberry (*Lonicera caerulea*)

Also known as: Edible honeysuckle, Blue honeysuckle, Haskap berry.

There are about two hundred species of honeysuckle, but very few have edible berries, and some may be poisonous, so you must make sure you've got one from a reliable source that is definitely sold as an edible honeyberry. This very hardy, perennial, deciduous shrub is a native of Siberia, northern China and northern Japan, with the modern cultivars being the result of work in the Soviet Union in the 1950s to produce reliably flavoursome berries.

Ornamental value

The oval leaves, from late winter or early spring until autumn, are green or grey-green, carried in pairs, sometimes slightly velvety, and about 2.5 inches (6 cm) long.

Small, creamy white or yellow flowers, paired and three-quarters of an inch (2 cm) long, recognisably those of honeysuckle, bloom quite briefly from February, March or April. A couple of months later the flowers would perhaps pass without much notice, but blooming so early in the year they are eye-catching and cheering. They're very attractive to bees, and coming out so early they are of great value to them, too.

The flowers are unusually cold-resistant, which means you're unlikely to lose the blooms, or the ensuing fruits, even in a harsh spring – though in fact I was told by the gardeners at one very experienced and famous demonstration garden that they routinely lost either the flowers or fruit of their honeyberry to late frosts. I take that as a reminder that nothing is guaranteed in gardening, because there are so many variables, and that what works for one gardener, or in one plot, may not work for another person, or in another place.

Different honeyberries grow to different sizes in maturity; the ones I've grown or seen, have all been around 4 feet (122 cm) tall and wide. They make a good, low hedge.

How to start

Honeyberry can be propagated from seed or cuttings, but to be absolutely certain you're getting the right species – and the right variety or cultivar for your garden – it's definitely best to start with container-grown plants from a nursery in spring. You need at least two plants, of more than one variety, to get a good crop of fruit. They are often sold as pairs of two types that are known to pollinate each other.

Growing

Plant your new honeyberry in spring, after the last frost, in any well-drained soil. Full sun is best for flowers and fruit, though they will tolerate partial shade. Young plants can suffer from strong winds, so give them a sheltered position if you can.

Fork over the ground to remove any perennial weeds, such as dandelions and couch grass. Dig a hole, and put the plant into it so that the rootball is slightly below the surface. Refill the hole with the soil you've dug out, firm it in with your boot, and give the area around the plant a throrough watering, even in wet soil. Spread a mulch of garden compost, old manure or a bought-in mulch such as bark, for a couple of feet (61 cm) around the plant. Put the plants

　　　　　　　　EAT YOUR FRONT GARDEN

at a spacing of 3 feet (1 m).

In future years, mulch the area every spring and again in autumn. Other than this I don't feed honeyberry as I'm wary of giving it too much nitrogen, which might lead to lush foliage and fewer flowers. But if you feel that the shrub isn't growing strongly, try spreading a handful of organic general fertiliser around the base each summer.

This is one shrub that does need watering in dry weather.

For me, honeyberry has never worked in containers, but some people succeed in growing them in large tubs. If grown in a container, honeyberry will need a lot of watering and more regular feeding.

Annual pruning isn't compulsory with this crop – only prune if you can actually see something that needs doing. This is carried out after harvesting the fruit. Remove any dead or broken branches, any weak, spindly growth, and overcrowded shoots which are crossing each other, or rubbing up against each other. You can encourage more flowering, and therefore more fruit, by 'tipping' – it just means cutting off the very tip of every shoot, or as many as you can manage, once a year immediately after harvest.

Problems

Pests and diseases are not commonly experienced with honeyberry, with the exception of birds, which in some gardens will take the ripe fruit. You could net the shrubs, but that would rather blow the invisibility of your invisible allotment. A lot of gardeners, including me, find that birds aren't much attracted to these blue berries, especially if the grower is quick to pick the fruit as soon as it's ripe.

In a cold, wet or windy spring there might not be enough insects around to pollinate the flowers. I've never had this trouble – I find early bumblebees work the plants very industriously – but if you don't see insects at the flowers, it could be worth hand-pollinating,

Fruit of Honeyberry (*Lonicera*)

by using a small, fine paintbrush to tickle each flower in turn, thus transferring pollen from one variety to the other.

Harvest & Storage

Apart from the fact that it will grow where blueberries won't, honeyberry is especially valued for the early ripening of its fruits, when little else is around. Mine are ready between late April to early June.

The berries are oblong, about a third of an inch (1 cm) long by half that across, and are ripe when they have a strong, blue-black colouring, and are dusted with a powdery or frosty white bloom. Bite one in half to be certain – the flesh should be dark in colour.

Honeyberry usually doesn't fruit until its second or third year; after that, when growing well, it can be quite prolific. The berries grow in clusters, but despite a strong colour contrast between fruit and leaves, they're not always that easy to spot – they grow underneath the foliage, which hides them somewhat, so you have to move the branches around with your hands to make sure you've got them all.

The fruits keep reasonably well in closed containers in the fridge, and can be frozen or dried.

Eating

Sweet – sometimes sweet and sour – honeyberries eaten raw have flavours of blackcurrant, honey, blueberry and blackberry. Use them wherever you would use any berry, especially blueberries, which they most resemble: in fruit salads, puddings, with cream and sugar, and as juice. My favourite use for them is in a mixed-fruit jam, where they add a really different and refreshing taste.

Fuchsia fruit and flowers

Fuchsia berries (*Fuchsia*)

Widely grown for its flowers in Britain – especially outside pubs, for some reason – this hardy or half-hardy, usually deciduous shrub is now slowly gaining popularity for its fruits.

Ornamental value

The long, pendant flowers, produced in numbers from summer until the first frosts of autumn, are waxy with pronounced stamens. Commonly bicoloured, the flowers are usually red and purple, but white, orange and blue are also seen. They are attractive to bees.

There's a wide choice of growing habits, with some suitable for hanging baskets, others for training as standards, using as ground cover or as a hedge, and many which can be kept as bushes.

How to start

All fuchsia berries are edible, but only some are palatable. Amongst those often recommended for fruit are the cultivar 'Fuchsiaberry', bred specifically to have large crops of big, tasty berries, 'Globosa', 'Jingle Bells', and the species *Fuchsia magellanica* and *F. splendens*. To maximise production of flowers and fruit, grow at least two different types.

Young plants are widely sold in the spring. When they arrive, pot them up in a small pot, in peat-free multipurpose compost, and keep them under cover for planting out after the last frost.

They're usually sold as hardy or half-hardy, but fuchsia hardiness varies from county to county, and even from garden to garden. Some half-hardy ones are worth taking a winter risk with, while some supposedly hardy ones are unreliably so.

As a genus, *Fuchsia* has a reputation for being very easy to propagate from cuttings, so it's not hard to give yourself some insurance against winter losses. In spring or early summer, select a healthy-looking shoot that's 3-4 inches (7.5-10 cm) long and has four sets of leaves on it. Cut it off just below a leaf node (the lump where the stalks of the leaves join the stem) with a sharp knife. Remove the two lower sets of leaves. Fill a 3 inch (7.5 cm) pot with peat-free multipurpose compost, and make a hole in the compost with a dibber, or a pencil. Put the cutting into the hole, so that the lowest leaves are only just above the compost. With your fingers, gently firm the compost around it so that it's held upright. Cover the whole pot with a plastic bag, using something like a plant label or a lolly stick to keep the plastic off the plant. Use a rubber band to close the bottom of the plastic loosely around the pot. Now put the pot in a warm place, but one that's out of direct sunlight. Keep the compost moist but not very wet. Within a couple of weeks, the cutting should have rooted – you'll be able to see small roots through the drainage holes in the bottom of the pot. Remove the bag. Once the new plant has plenty of roots, and there is no further danger of frost, it's ready to plant out.

GROWING

Fuchsias want sun, but they will thrive best in a position where they have some shade during the hottest part of the day – in other words from about noon to teatime. Any soil that's well-drained and reasonably fertile will do.

Dig a hole in the ground and put the plant in it so that the base

Fuchsia

of its stem is about 2 inches (5 cm) below soil level. Give it a spacing from its neighbours of at least a foot (30 cm).

Other than the very largest fuchsias, most are suitable for growing in containers of peat-free multipurpose compost, planted the same way as if in the ground. The pot should be at least 15 inches (38 cm) deep and wide. 'Fuchsiaberry' grows particularly well in pots.

Regular watering throughout spring and summer is advisable for fuchsias, and a feed with a proprietary seaweed solution in late summer can boost the crop.

There are various methods of pruning hardy fuchsias for different results, but the simplest rule to follow, at least until you get used to growing them, is this: just as the new growth appears in spring, cut all the old growth right back to immediately above the new shoots.

Fuchsias which aren't fully hardy are best kept in pots, so that you can move them to a cool, frost free place before the first frost of autumn. At the end of winter they'll look as if they're dead, but they're probably not: in about March, with luck, you'll see tiny new leaf shoots appearing on the stems. Prune the old stems back – again, stopping just above the new growth – and water the plant lightly using a fine rose on a watering can. They can go back out after the last frost.

If you live in an area with cold autumns, even supposedly hardy fuchsias will benefit from a mulch of straw to keep frost off their roots.

In late April and again in late May, pinch out – that is, remove with your fingernails or a knife – the topmost pair of leaves from each shoot. This will encourage bushiness and free flowering.

PROBLEMS

There are quite a few pests and diseases which can occasionally attack fuchsias, but for the most part, grown outdoors under normal conditions, they go untroubled.

HARVEST & STORAGE

Fruiting time varies, but it'll usually be from late summer into the autumn. The berries are in most cases about an inch (2.5 cm) long, and purple when ripe. Ripeness is not easily judged; the fruits will be slightly softer, and slightly deeper in colour than before, but tasting them is really the only way to be certain. If they taste good, they're ready – unripe fuchsia berries are not pleasant. They can be dried or frozen, or kept in a plastic box in the fridge for about a week.

EATING

The taste of the berries (like everything else about fuchsias) varies, but flavours such as fig, citrus, grape and kiwi fruit are often mentioned. Some have a pleasantly peppery aftertaste. They are very juicy.

They are at their best, I think, in jam, but can also be eaten raw or used in recipes calling for blueberries or grapes. The flowers are also edible, but without much flavour.

SECTION SIX

RESOURCES

A selection of seed & plant suppliers

Most seed and plant catalogues stock most seeds and plants. But when I'm after something a bit out of the ordinary, these are some of the websites I turn to:

Chiltern Seeds (www.chilternseeds.co.uk).
Heritage Seed Library (www.gardenorganic.org.uk/hsl).
Lubera (www.lubera.co.uk).
Nicky's Nursery (www.nickys-nursery.co.uk).
Pennard Plants (www.pennardplants.com).
Plants of Distinction (www.plantsofdistinction.co.uk).
Real Seeds (www.realseeds.co.uk).
Thomas Etty Esq (www.thomasetty.co.uk).
Victoriana (www.victoriananursery.co.uk).

Sundries suppliers

These days there are a lot of peat-free composts available – and some of them are really terrible. Disappointingly, price does sometimes count: the cheapest are often the worst. I've tried every one of them over the years, and while I would recommend that you experiment yourself the two products I currently use are Vegro Seed Compost, and coir bricks, which come as dried and compressed blocks that you soak in water to turn them into compost. Both are sold by a company called Fertile Fibre, at www.fertilefibre.com.

When I mention 'sand' in this book, I'm referring to a product called horticultural sand, which is widely sold in bags in garden centres, DIY shops and online. Mixed with seed or peat-free multipurpose compost it improves the drainage, and it's also used for storing crops, especially roots and tubers, over winter.

Most people who've been gardening for a while have far more plastic pots than they will ever need – and they're not all that easy to get rid of, without actually putting them in the bin. So, before you buy any, consider trying to get some free from friends, or ask for them on social media and places like Freecycle.

The 'Green Bags' I refer to are a special type of reusable polythene bag designed to keep fruit and vegetables fresh for weeks, rather than days. I've been using them for at least twenty years, and find them indispensable: they cut food waste, even during gluts, to an absolute minimum. They come in several sizes and these days are widely available, for instance from the kitchen goods supplier, Lakeland (www.lakeland.co.uk), where they are listed under the name 'Stayfresh longer bags'.

FURTHER READING

Around the World in 80 Plants, Stephen Barstow (Permanent Publications, 2014).
The Cultivariable Growing Guide, William Whitson (Cultivariable, 2015).
Growing Unusual Vegetables, Simon Hickmott (Eco-Logic Books, 2003).
How to Grow Perennial Vegetables, Martin Crawford (Green Books, 2012).
Incredible Edibles, Matthew Biggs (Dorling Kindersley, 2018).
Oriental Vegetables, Joy Larkcom (Kodansha International, 2008).
Perennial Vegetables, Eric Toensmeier (Chelsea Green, 2007).
Plants for a Future, Ken Fern (Permanent Publications, 1997).
Rare Vegetables for Garden and Table, John Organ (Faber & Faber, 1960).
Quinces: Growing and Cooking, Jane McMorland Hunter and Sue Dunster (Prospect Books, 2014).

INDEX

Achira (*Canna*), 33
Allium tuberosum, 55-61
amaranth (*Amaranthus*), 45-53
Amaranthus, 45-53
Andean crops, 139, 149, 197
anu (*Tropaeolum tuberosum*), 139
Apios americana, 151-7
artichoke substitute, 66, 67, 149, 188
Aslet, Ken, 140
asparagus substitutes, 22, 128, 169, 181, 211
Atriplex hortensis, 103-5
au gratin dishes, 67
Aztecs, 45

bamboo (*Phyllostachys*), 87-91
Barstow, Stephen, 165, 210, 235
bats-in-the-belfry *(Campanula),* 69
bees, 13, 39, 56, 70, 185, 192, 205, 215, 221, 223, 227
beefsteak plant (*Perilla frutescens*), 93
bellflower *(Campanula),* 69
birds, 35, 50, 58, 63, 65, 83, 173, 215, 223
black caraway (*Bunium bulbocastanum*), 99
black cumin (*Bunium bulbocastanum*), 99
bladder campion (*Silene vulgaris*), 75, 76
blackfly, 59, 145, 193
blanching, 58, 67
blueberry substitutes, 225, 231
blue honeysuckle (*Lonicera caerulea*), 221
bubbolini (*Silene vulgaris*), 75
Bunium bulbocastanum, 99-101
butterflies, 76, 145, 193

cakes & confectionary, 53
calendar, gardening, 9

callaloo (*Amaranthus*), 45, 46
Campanula, 69-73
Canna, 33-7
capers substitute, 194-5
casseroles, 22, 37, 52, 149, 189
caterpillars, 145, 146, 193
Caucasian spinach (*Hablitzia*), 165-9
celery substitutes, 66, 134
cellophane noodles, 36
cereal, breakfast, 52
Chaenomeles, 215-9
cheese dishes, 60, 129, 195
cheese flower (*Malva*), 39
'cheeses', mallow (*Malva*), 42, 43
cheeses, fruit, 219
Chinese artichoke (*Stachys affinis*), 185
Chinese chives (*Allium tuberosum*), 55
Chinese leek (*Allium tuberosum*), 55
Chinese water celery (*Oenanthe javanica*), 131-5
Chinese yam (*Dioscorea batatas*), 8, 159-163
chitting, 198
chop suey greens (*Glebionis coronaria*), 107-11
chorogi (*Stachys affinis*), 185
chufa (*Cyperus esculentus*), 113, 114, 116,
Chrysanthemum see Glebionis coronaria
cinnamon vine (*Dioscorea batatas*), 8, 159, 162
climbing spinach (*Hablitzia*), 165
cloches, home-made mini, 95
comfrey, 42
compost:
    checking moistness of, 41, 122-3

suppliers, 234
Crithmum maritimum, 121-9
crosnes (Stachys affinis), 185-9
crown daisy (Glebionis coronaria), 107
crumble (topping), 53
cumin substitutes, 96, 101
Cyperus esculentus, 113-9

Dahlia, 13-23
dancing crane (Zingiber mioga), 81
daylily (Hemerocallis), 25-31
Dioscorea batatas, 8, 159-163
ditch lily (Hemerocallis), 25
dolmades (stuffed leaves), 43, 175, 181
drainage of soil, testing, 124
drought-tolerant plants, 28, 47, 57, 64,
    124-5, 169, 179
drying food for storage, 50, 117, 128
dumplings, 61

earth almond (Cyperus esculentus), 113
earth chestnut (Bunium bulbocastanum),
    99-101
earth nut (Bunium bulbocastanum), 99
edible chrysanthemum (Glebionis
    coronaria), 107
edible honeysuckle (Lonicera caerulea), 221
egg dishes, 77, 96, 129, 211
elephant head (Amaranthus), 45

fermented foods, 43, 175, 189
Flamingo (Oenanthe javanica), 131-2
flat chives (Allium tuberosum), 55
flour, 53, 76, 157,
flowering chives (Allium tuberosum), 55
flowering quince (Chaenomeles), 215
flowers (edible), 23, 26, 39, 43, 63-4, 97,
    111, 149, 191, 193, 195, 231

French spinach (Atriplex hortensis), 103
Fuchsia, 227-31
fungal diseases, 42, 59, 174

gao choy (Allium tuberosum), 55
garland chrysanthemum (Glebionis
    coronaria), 107
garlic chives (Allium tuberosum), 55-60
giboshi (Hosta), 205
ginger see Zingiber mioga
Glebionis coronaria, 107-111
gluten-free, 45
golden chives (Allium tuberosum), 55,
    58, 60, 61
golden needles (Hemerocallis), 25, 27, 31
gow choy (Allium tuberosum), 55
grape leaves (Vitis), 171
grasses (ornamental), 114
'green bags', 148, 235
greens (plants eaten as), 43, 66, 76-7,
    109-11, 134, 211
grit, horticultural, 40, 125,
ground cover, 100, 131, 145, 185-6, 191,
    197, 215, 227
groundnut (Apios americana), 151, 154, 156
gum zum (Hemerocallis), 25

Hablitzia, 165-9
harebell (Campanula), 69
haskap berry (Lonicera caerulea), 221
Helianthus annuus, 63-6
Hemerocallis, 25-31
hodoimo (Apios americana), 151
honeyberry (Lonicera caerulea), 221-5
hop shoots (Humulus lupulus), 177-81
Hosta, 205-211
hoverflies, 56, 99, 107, 192
huang hua cai (Hemerocallis), 25

Humulus lupulus, 177-81

Indian cress (*Tropaeolum majus*), 191
Indian potato (*Apios americana*), 151
Indian shot plant (*Canna*), 33
inulin, 23
invisible allotment, 8-9, 19, 46, 166, 223

jams, jellies & marmalades, 219, 225, 231
Japanese ginger (*Zingiber mioga*), 81-5
Japanese parsley (*Oenanthe javanica*), 131
Japanese quince (*Chaenomeles*), 215-9
Japonica (*Chaenomeles*), 215
jin zhen cai (*Hemerocallis*), 25
jiu cai (*Allium tuberosum*), 55

kitten test, the, 145
kiwicha (*Amaranthus*), 45
knot root (*Stachys affinis*), 185

layering for propagation, 179
lettuce substitutes, 43, 69, 105
Lonicera caerulea, 221-5
love-lies-bleeding (*Amaranthus*), 45-7

machua (*Tropaeolum tuberosum*), 139
maidenstears (*Silene vulgaris*), 75
mallow (*Malva*), 39-43
Malva, 39-43
mash, 22, 73, 119, 157, 163
mashua (*Tropaeolum tuberosum*), 139-49
Maule's quince (*Chaenomeles*), 215
mice, 66, 116, 117, 160, 174
mioga (*Zingiber mioga*), 81
mock quince (*Chaenomeles*), 215, 217, 219
mountain spinach (*Atriplex hortensis*), 103
mulching, 28, 36, 57-8, 83, 88, 95, 109, 144, 146, 161, 172, 179, 187, 199, 208-9,

222-3, 230
Myoga (*Zingiber mioga*), 81, 85

nasturtium (*Tropaeolum majus*), 191-5
New Zealand yam (*Oxalis tuberosa*), 197
nira (*Allium tuberosum*), 55
noodles, 36, 60, 61
nut grass (*Cyperus esculentus*), 113

oca (*Oxalis tuberosa*), 197-203
Oenanthe javanica, 131-5
orach (*Atriplex hortensis*), 103-5
oriental garlic (*Allium tuberosum),* 55
Oxalis tuberosa, 197-203

parsley substitutes, 22, 96, 101, 129, 134, 181
pasta dishes, 77, 96, 111, 195
Perilla frutescens, 93-7
Phyllostachys, 87-91
pickles, 85, 90, 97, 111, 126, 128, 129, 175, 181, 189, 194, 210
pies, 22, 73, 91
pignut (*Bunium bulbocastanum*), 99
pigweed (*Amaranthus*), 45
pinching out, 93, 230
plantain lilies (*Hosta*), 205
plant suppliers, 234
pollinating by hand, 223
pond plants, 114, 131
potato bean (*Apios americana*), 151
potato substitutes, 22, 37, 149, 156-7, 161, 163, 203
pots, sources of, 235
prince's feather (*Amaranthus*), 45
propagation, 16, 26, 28, 34, 76, 82, 87, 95, 108, 132, 152, 160, 166, 206, 222, 228

Queensland arrowroot (*Canna*), 33
quince *see Chaenomeles*

radish substitutes, 23, 73, 149, 188
rampion (*Campanula*), 69, 70, 72-3
rapunzel (*Campanula*), 69
rats, 174
red orach (*Atriplex hortensis*), 103-5
replant perennials, 114, 139
rice:
  dishes, 23, 52, 66, 96, 111, 134, 195
  substitutes, 52, 163
rock garden plants, 55, 121
rock samphire (*Crithmum maritimum*),
  121-9
rush nut (*Cyperus esculentus*), 113
rust (fungal disease), 42, 59

salads, 22, 23, 31, 43, 53, 61, 66, 69, 73,
  77, 85, 91, 96, 105, 111, 129, 134, 169,
  175, 181, 189, 191, 195, 210
samphire (*Crithmum maritimum*), 121-9
sand, horticultural, 22, 71, 122, 148, 234
sandwiches, 60, 135, 195
Scandinavian spinach (*Hablitzia*), 165
scented plants, 69, 76, 107, 151, 153, 181,
  205, 219, 240
sculpit (*Silene vulgaris*), 75, 76
sea fennel (*Crithmum maritimum*), 121
seaside gardens, plants suitable for,
  104, 121, 124
seed suppliers, 234
shade, plants suitable for, 18, 27, 39, 57,
  70, 72, 88, 108, 168, 192, 204, 205,
  207, 216, 222, 228
shiso (*Perilla frutescens*), 93
shungiku (*Glebionis coronaria*), 107,
  108, 111

Silene inflata see *S.vulgaris*
Silene vulgaris, 75-7
Slug Rings, 209
slugs & snails, 20, 35, 58, 66, 72, 83, 109,
  140, 144, 146, 147, 200, 207, 208-9
soups, 31, 37, 43, 52, 60, 61, 73, 85, 91, 96,
  105, 111, 134, 149, 157, 163, 181, 189, 195,
  203, 211
spinach substitutes, *see* greens
Stachys affinis, 185-9
stews, 22, 31, 37, 52, 91, 96, 149, 157, 163, 203
stir-fries, 31, 61, 85, 90, 111, 129, 189
stridolo (*Silene vulgaris*), 75-7
stuffed leaves, *see* dolmades
sunflower see *Helianthus annuus*
sushi, 85, 97, 211
sweet dishes, 22, 52, 53, 96, 149, 225

tempura, 85, 97, 211
tiger nuts (*Cyperus esculentus*), 113-9
tipping, 223
Tropaeolum majus, 191-5
Tropaeolum tuberosum, 139-49
tuberous nasturtium (*Tropaeolum
  tuberosum*), 139

urui (*Hosta*), 205
USDA Hardiness Zones, 9

variegated water dropwort (*Oenanthe
  javanica*), 131
vine leaves (*Vitis*), 171-5
vine weevil, 200
Vitis, 171-5

wall plants, 121, 124-6, 168, 215
water celery (*Oenanthe javanica*), 131-5
window boxes, 7

winnowing, 50, 51
winter, plants useful in, 25, 58, 65, 69, 72, 99, 101, 109, 122, 134, 154, 169, 187

yam (*Dioscorea batatas*), 8, 159-63
yellow flower vegetable (*Hemerocallis*), 25
yellow nutsedge (*Cyperus esculentus*), 113

Zingiber mioga, 81-5